HONG KONG
TRAVEL GUIDE
2025

"Discover the Finest Accommodations, Best Times to Visit, Must-See Attractions in Hong Kong, and Much More Essential Information."

TABLE OF CONTENTS

Cultural Experiences

Temple Street Night Market
Man Mo Temple
Wong Tai Sin Temple
Chi Lin Nunnery
Ten Thousand Buddhas Monastery
Hong Kong Museum of History

Chapter 5.

Outdoor Adventures

Lantau Island and Ngong Ping Village
Dragon's Back Hike
Sai Kung Peninsula and Geopark
Hong Kong Park
Tai O Fishing Village

Chapter 6.

Culinary Delights

Dim Sum restaurants
Street food favorites
Michelin-starred dining experiences
Traditional Cantonese cuisine
Tea culture in Hong Kong

Chapter 7.

Practical Information

Transportation options (MTR, buses, trams)
Airport transfers
Recommended accommodations (hotels, hostels, guesthouses)
Currency and banking
Safety tips and emergency contacts

Chapter 8.

Shopping and Entertainment

Causeway Bay shopping district
Mong Kok markets
Luxury shopping in Central
Nightlife hotspots
Cultural performances and events

Chapter 9.

Day Trips and Excursions

Macau day trip
Shenzhen day trip
Outlying islands (Lamma Island, Cheung Chau)
Historical sites in New Territories

Chapter 10.

<u>Conclusion and Additional Resources</u>

Final thoughts on visiting Hong Kong
Useful websites and apps for travelers
Further reading and references

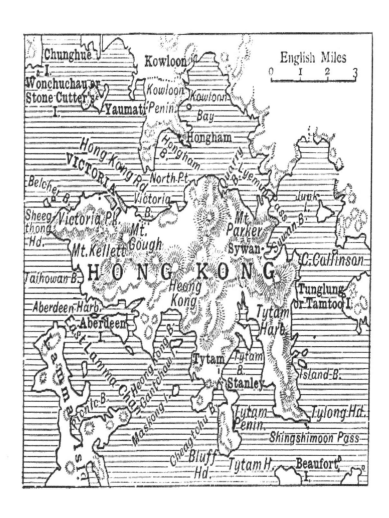

INTRODUCTION

Dazzling metropolis, Hong Kong seamlessly blends Eastern charm with Western influence, creating a captivating fusion of culture, commerce, and history. Nestled on China's southeastern coast, this dynamic city-state boasts towering skyscrapers, bustling markets, and breathtaking natural landscapes.

From Humble Beginnings to Global Powerhouse

Once a small fishing village, Hong Kong has transformed into a global force. It thrives on one of the world's busiest ports and a booming financial center. This strategic location and vibrant economy have attracted people from all corners of the globe, weaving a rich tapestry of languages, cuisines, and traditions.

A City of Contrasts

Visitors are greeted by a mesmerizing skyline dominated by glittering skyscrapers, like the iconic International Commerce Centre and the striking Bank of China Tower. Yet, amidst the urban energy, tranquil havens await. Explore serene parks and gardens, secluded beaches, or verdant hiking trails, offering a welcome escape from the city's buzz.

Immerse Yourself in the Vibe

Central's narrow alleys offer a unique experience. Traditional tea houses stand side-by-side with trendy cocktail bars. In Mong Kok's bustling markets, immerse yourself in a sensory overload as vendors hawk everything from exotic spices to the latest gadgets. And don't forget to tantalize your taste buds with a delectable array of culinary delights, from mouthwatering dim sum to fiery Sichuan hotpot.

Beyond the Skyline: A Place Steeped in Tradition

Hong Kong offers more than just skyscrapers and shopping malls. It's a place where ancient traditions co-exist with modern life. Discover centuries-old temples nestled amidst towering buildings, or witness the age-old practice of tai chi in one of the city's many parks.

Unforgettable Experiences Await

Whether you seek exhilarating nightlife, cultural immersion, or simply a breathtaking view, Hong Kong caters to every traveler. Join us as we explore this enchanting city, where every corner reveals a new adventure and every experience leaves a lasting impression.

CHAPTER ONE

MY TRAVEL EXPERIENCE

The humid air of Hong Kong hit me like a warm welcome as I disembarked from the plane. Stepping into the bustling chaos of the airport, I knew this wouldn't be your typical vacation. Excitement crackled in the air, a promise of adventures waiting around every corner.

My journey began with a skyward ascent to Victoria Peak. As the tram climbed the steep incline, the urban sprawl unfolded beneath me. Towering skyscrapers pierced the clouds, their glass facades reflecting the morning sun. But nestled amidst the concrete jungle were pockets of emerald green – a reminder of Hong Kong's surprising natural beauty. Reaching the peak, I was greeted by a panorama that stole my breath away. The city stretched out endlessly, a mesmerizing dance of modern marvels and timeless mountains.

Next, I plunged headfirst into the heart of Kowloon. Mong Kok's street markets were a sensory overload in the best way possible. A kaleidoscope of colors assaulted my eyes, from the vibrant displays of exotic fruits to the neon signs that buzzed with an electric energy. The air was thick with the aroma of sizzling street food – a tantalizing invitation to indulge. I wandered through the maze-like alleys, my curiosity piqued by everything from steaming bowls of wonton noodles to the fragrant puffs of freshly made egg waffles. Each bite was an explosion of flavor, a unique taste of Hong Kong's culinary diversity.

Seeking a serene counterpoint to the bustling streets, I ventured to the tranquil oasis of Man Mo Temple. Stepping through the ornately carved gates, a sense of peace descended upon me. The air hung heavy with the scent of burning incense, and intricate deities watched over me with serene smiles. It was a sanctuary in the heart of the city, a place to reflect and appreciate the rich cultural heritage of Hong Kong.

But what truly left an indelible mark were the people. From the friendly shopkeepers who patiently helped me bargain for souvenirs to the locals who offered insightful directions despite the language barrier, I felt a sense of warmth and community. Their resilience and entrepreneurial spirit were contagious, a testament to the city's vibrant pulse. Sharing a bowl of steaming congee with a group of strangers, I found myself drawn into lively conversations, a testament to the welcoming nature of the Hong Kong people.

As twilight painted the sky in hues of orange and purple, I found myself gliding across Victoria Harbour on a traditional junk boat. The city skyline transformed into a dazzling display of lights, a symphony of color that mirrored the energy of Hong Kong itself. In that perfect moment, I felt a deep appreciation for this place of contrasts – where ancient traditions thrived alongside modern marvels, and where the past seamlessly blended with the future.

Leaving Hong Kong was bittersweet. Yet, as my journey came to a close, I carried with me a treasure trove of memories. From the awe-inspiring heights of Victoria Peak to the bustling depths of its street markets, Hong Kong had woven its magic spell. It was a city of contradictions and enchantments, a place that had captured my heart and left me yearning to return someday.

Personal account of your time in Hong Kong

My first taste of Hong Kong was the electric buzz of the International Airport. Stepping off the plane, I was instantly swept up in a whirlwind of energy – a fitting introduction to this vibrant metropolis. Towering skyscrapers dominated the cityscape as I ventured into Central, their reflections shimmering on the bustling streets below. Neon signs flickered, and the cacophony of street vendors hawking their wares created a symphony of sights and sounds. The aroma of sizzling street food filled the air, a tantalizing invitation to explore Hong Kong's diverse culinary scene.

Ascending Victoria Peak was a must. From the iconic Peak Tower, the city sprawled out before me like a glittering jewel box. Towering skyscrapers danced with the clouds, while pockets of emerald green peeked through the urban landscape, a testament to Hong Kong's captivating blend of modern marvel and natural beauty.

But Hong Kong's heart truly lies with its people. Warm smiles and helpful directions from strangers created a welcoming atmosphere wherever I went. Sharing steaming bowls of wonton noodles with locals sparked lively conversations, offering glimpses into the city's vibrant soul.

Temple Street Night Market was an experience in itself. Narrow alleyways overflowed with vendors, their colorful displays a feast for the eyes. The air crackled with energy as I bargained for souvenirs, the thrill of the hunt adding to the market's unique charm.

Amidst the urban chaos, moments of serenity awaited. Nan Lian Garden offered a tranquil escape. Meticulously manicured bonsai trees adorned the landscape, while lotus ponds reflected the serenity of the space. Here, I found a welcome respite, a chance to savor the peacefulness amidst the city's constant hum.

As I departed Hong Kong, a kaleidoscope of memories swirled through my mind. From the breathtaking views of Victoria Peak to the vibrant energy of the night markets, the city had woven its magic spell. It was a symphony of sights, sounds, and flavors, a place where the past and present collided in a mesmerizing dance. Hong Kong had captured a piece of my heart, leaving behind an indelible mark and a yearning to return someday.

Highlights and memorable moments

Victoria Peak's summit offered a breathtaking sunset panorama, painting the city skyline in a fiery glow. Temple Street Night Market, a maze of colorful displays and sizzling aromas, presented endless opportunities for bargaining and delectable street food discoveries. Nan Lian Garden provided a tranquil escape, its meticulously manicured landscapes offering a welcome respite from the urban buzz.

Sailing across Victoria Harbour on a traditional junk boat, I witnessed the city's skyline transform into a dazzling display of lights. Immersed in the rich cultural heritage at Man Mo Temple, the fragrant incense and intricate deities transported me back in time. A leisurely stroll along the Avenue of Stars' picturesque waterfront promenade allowed me to savor the harbor's stunning views.

Indulging in a sumptuous dim sum feast at a traditional tea house was a culinary adventure, each delicate dumpling and savory dish a delightful surprise. The scenic Dragon's Back trail on Hong Kong Island offered panoramic views of the coastline and surrounding islands, a perfect escape into nature. Riding the iconic Star Ferry across Victoria Harbour, the cool breeze carried the city's sights and sounds, creating a memorable experience.

The mesmerizing Symphony of Lights show from the Tsim Sha Tsui waterfront was a highlight, the choreographed display of lights and music painting the skyline in a magical spectacle. These experiences capture the essence of my captivating journey through Hong Kong, a treasure trove of memories I'll forever cherish.

Victoria Peak's summit unveiled a breathtaking sunset panorama, the city skyline ablaze with fiery hues. Temple Street Night Market, a labyrinth of vibrant displays and mouthwatering aromas, offered endless opportunities for haggling and indulging in delectable street food. Nan Lian Garden's meticulous landscaping provided a tranquil sanctuary amidst the urban energy.

Sailing across Victoria Harbour on a traditional junk boat, I witnessed the city's skyline transform into a dazzling display of lights. Man Mo Temple, steeped in rich cultural heritage, transported me back in time with its fragrant incense and intricate deities. A leisurely stroll along the Avenue of Stars' picturesque waterfront promenade allowed me to savor the harbor's stunning vistas.

Indulging in a sumptuous dim sum feast at a traditional tea house was a culinary journey, each delicate dumpling and savory dish a delightful surprise. The scenic Dragon's Back trail offered a welcome escape into nature, showcasing panoramic views of the coastline and surrounding islands. Riding the iconic Star Ferry across Victoria Harbour, the cool breeze carried the city's sights and sounds, creating a lasting memory.

The Tsim Sha Tsui waterfront came alive with the mesmerizing Symphony of Lights show, the choreographed display of lights and music weaving a magical spectacle on the skyline. These experiences capture the essence of my captivating journey through Hong Kong, a treasure trove of memories I'll forever cherish.

But Hong Kong offered so much more:

Exploring the historic charm of Sheung Wan and Central, with their colonial architecture and trendy cafes.

Riding the Ngong Ping 360 cable car to Lantau Island, encountering the majestic Tian Tan Buddha and exploring the tranquil Ngong Ping Village.

Tsim Sha Tsui East's picturesque promenade offered stunning views of Victoria Harbour and the Hong Kong skyline, perfect for a leisurely stroll.

Mong Kok's vibrant markets presented a unique opportunity to sample a wide variety of street food delicacies, from the adventurous stinky tofu to freshly grilled seafood.

Immersing myself in the rich cultural heritage through a traditional Cantonese opera performance at the iconic Sunbeam Theatre.

The Hong Kong Museum of History's fascinating exhibits provided insights into the city's rich and diverse past.

The historic Peak Tram offered a thrilling ride to Victoria Peak, where the city sprawled out below in a mesmerizing panorama.

PMQ (formerly Police Married Quarters) unveiled hidden gems and local treasures at its quirky boutiques and art galleries.

The electrifying atmosphere of Happy Valley Racecourse was a sensory experience, buzzing with excitement as I watched the famous horse races.

Ending my trip with a traditional Chinese tea ceremony allowed me to savor the delicate flavors of fine teas, reflecting on my unforgettable adventures in Hong Kong.

Hong Kong, a tapestry of experiences, left me with a kaleidoscope of memories, a yearning to return and explore even more.

CHAPTER TWO

GETTING TO KNOW HONG KONG

A Land of Diverse Districts

Hong Kong, a vibrant metropolis nestled on China's southeastern coast, is comprised of three distinct areas: Hong Kong Island, Kowloon Peninsula, and the New Territories. Each district boasts its own unique personality, offering a diverse range of experiences for travelers.

Hong Kong Island: Home to the central business district, this island pulsates with energy. Towering skyscrapers pierce the sky, casting shadows over luxury shopping malls and bustling nightlife districts.

Kowloon Peninsula: Across Victoria Harbour lies Kowloon, renowned for its frenetic energy. Explore labyrinthine markets overflowing with treasures, savor delectable cuisine from around the world, or simply soak in the captivating panorama of Hong Kong Island's skyline.

The New Territories: Craving a respite from the urban jungle? Venture to the New Territories. Lush countrysides, scenic hiking trails, and traditional villages offer a glimpse into a more serene side of Hong Kong.

Climate and Perfect Timing

Hong Kong boasts a subtropical climate, characterized by hot and humid summers (May to September) and mild winters (December to February). The ideal time to visit is during the fall and early winter (October to December). The weather is comfortable for exploring, and the crowds haven't quite reached their peak. Be prepared for occasional rain showers year-round, especially during the wet season (May to September).

Language and Communication

Cantonese and English are the official languages of Hong Kong. While Cantonese dominates daily life, English is prevalent in tourist areas, hotels, and restaurants. Learning a few basic Cantonese phrases (greetings, thank you) goes a long way and demonstrates respect for the local culture.

Money Matters

The official currency is the Hong Kong Dollar (HKD). ATMs are readily available throughout the city, and credit cards are widely accepted at most establishments. It's wise to carry a combination of cash and credit cards for convenience, particularly when visiting smaller shops or street markets.

Safety First

Hong Kong is generally a safe city with low crime rates. However, staying vigilant is essential, especially in crowded areas. Be mindful of your belongings and avoid displaying valuables openly. For emergencies, dial 999 for police, fire, or medical assistance. Non-emergency inquiries can be directed to the 24-hour Visitor Hotline at 99999, where multilingual staff can provide information and support.

Geography and districts

Hong Kong, a captivating metropolis, unfolds on the southeastern coast of China. This Special Administrative Region (SAR) encompasses a mosaic of landscapes, each offering a distinct experience.

Hong Kong Island: The Heart of the City

Thrumming with energy, Hong Kong Island forms the core of the city. Here, towering skyscrapers pierce the sky, housing the central business district and government offices. Luxury shopping malls and iconic landmarks line the northern shores, while the island's southern coast offers a welcome contrast. Scenic hiking trails weave through lush greenery, and pristine beaches beckon with opportunities for relaxation. Upscale residential neighborhoods provide a glimpse into a life of luxury amidst the urban buzz.

Kowloon Peninsula: A Bustling Tapestry

Directly across Victoria Harbour lies Kowloon Peninsula, a district renowned for its frenetic energy. Immerse yourself in the labyrinthine markets overflowing with treasures, savor delectable cuisine from around the world, or simply stand mesmerized by the captivating panorama of Hong Kong Island's skyline. Tsim Sha Tsui, a vibrant district teeming with tourists, offers world-class shopping, cultural attractions like the Avenue of Stars, and breathtaking views of the city.

The New Territories: A Serene Escape

Yearning for a respite from the urban jungle? The New Territories provide a tranquil escape. This region, the largest and least densely populated, boasts a diverse range of landscapes. Lush countrysides unfold, perfect for exploration on foot or by bicycle. Hiking trails weave through verdant hills, offering opportunities to commune with nature. Traditional villages, steeped in history, provide a glimpse into a slower pace of life. Explore historic temples, marvel at ancient fortresses, and immerse yourself in the rich cultural heritage of the area.

Outlying Islands: A World Beyond

Beyond the main territory, over 200 outlying islands beckon with their unique charm. Lantau Island, the largest and most visited, stuns with its scenic beauty. Ascend Ngong Ping 360 cable car for breathtaking views, encounter the majestic Tian Tan Buddha, or explore the serenity of Po Lin Monastery. Family-friendly attractions like Hong Kong Disneyland offer a world of wonder for all ages.

A Tapestry of Experiences

Hong Kong's geography is a captivating blend of urban sophistication, natural wonders, and cultural treasures. Each district unveils a distinct facet of this vibrant city. Whether you crave the heart-pumping energy of Kowloon's markets or the tranquility of the New Territories' landscapes, Hong Kong offers a diverse tapestry of experiences waiting to be explored.

Climate and best times to visit

Hong Kong's charm unfolds across four distinct seasons, each offering a unique twist on your experience. The city basks in a subtropical climate, transitioning from hot and humid summers to mild and pleasant winters.

Spring: A Time of Blossoming (March to May)

Spring paints Hong Kong in a canvas of comfortable warmth. With temperatures ranging from 18°C to 26°C (64°F to 79°F), it's ideal for outdoor adventures. Explore scenic hiking trails or embark on sightseeing expeditions without breaking a sweat. The skies are generally clear, and occasional rain showers cleanse the city, leaving it fresh and vibrant.

Summer: Embrace the Vibrancy (June to August)

Summer arrives with a burst of heat and humidity. Temperatures soar above 30°C (86°F), and the air thickens with moisture. While the city pulsates with life, outdoor activities can be less appealing. However, if you don't mind the warmth, this is the season for the lowest hotel rates. Be prepared for frequent rain showers and occasional typhoons, which may disrupt travel plans.

Autumn: The Ideal Embrace (September to November)

Autumn emerges as the undisputed champion for visiting Hong Kong. The weather transitions to a state of pure bliss, with mild temperatures ranging from 22°C to

28°C (72°F to 82°F) and comfortable humidity levels. Sunny skies bathe the city in a warm glow, making it perfect for exploring every corner. Hike through verdant landscapes, embark on cultural excursions, or simply relax outdoors and soak in the delightful atmosphere. This season also coincides with vibrant festivals like the Mid-Autumn Festival and the Chung Yeung Festival, offering a glimpse into local traditions.

Winter: A Touch of Cool (December to February)

Winter ushers in a wave of pleasant coolness. Average temperatures hover between 15°C to 20°C (59°F to 68°F), making it comfortable for sightseeing without feeling overwhelmed by heat. The skies tend to be clear, offering breathtaking views, and rainfall is minimal. While evenings can get a little chilly, pack a light jacket and continue exploring the city's magic.

The Perfect Timing

For an experience that blends outdoor adventures with cultural immersion, autumn (September to November) and winter (December to February) present the perfect opportunities. Pleasant weather and clear skies make exploring a joy, while festive celebrations add a touch of local flavor. Spring (March to May) offers a good alternative, but be prepared for occasional rain. Summer (June to August) is generally the least favorable time due to the heat and humidity. However, if you can brave the elements, you'll be rewarded with lower hotel rates.

So, pack your bags based on the season that best suits your preferences, and get ready to discover the captivating allure of Hong Kong!

Language and communication tips

Hong Kong, a vibrant tapestry of cultures, boasts two official languages: Cantonese and English. While Cantonese dominates daily conversations, English remains prevalent in tourist areas, hotels, and restaurants. Here's how to navigate communication and embrace the local spirit:

Cantonese Gems:

Learning a few basic Cantonese phrases goes a long way. Here are some useful ones:

- **Greetings:** Hello - 你好 (néih hóu), Goodbye - 再見 (joi gin)
- **Courtesy:** Thank you - 多謝 (dō jeh), Please/Excuse me - 唔該 (m`h gōi), Sorry - 對唔住 (deui m`h jyuh)
- **Essentials:** Yes - 係 (hái), No - 唔係 (m`h hái)
- **Getting By:** Do you speak English? - 你識唔識講英文? (néih sīk m`h sīk góng yīng màhn?), How much is this? - 呢個幾錢? (níh gǒ gēi chín?), Where is the restroom? - 洗手間喺邊度? (sái sáu gaan hái bīn dou?)

English for Ease:

English remains a valuable tool for communication. Here are some common phrases:

- Greetings, Thank you, Excuse me, Please, Sorry
- Do you speak English?
- Where is [destination]?
- How much is this?
- Can you help me?

Respecting Local Customs:

Hong Kong is a melting pot of cultures. Remember to:

- Remove shoes before entering homes, a sign of respect.
- Address people with titles (Mr., Mrs., Miss).
- Be mindful in temples and shrines - dress modestly and avoid disruptive behavior.

English on Display:

English signage is widely used in tourist areas, on menus, and in information materials.

Bridging the Gap:

Translation apps and bilingual staff at hotels, restaurants, and attractions are readily available.

Hong Kong, a vibrant tapestry of cultures, thrives on communication. While Cantonese reigns supreme,

English serves as a valuable tool, especially in tourist areas. Here's how to navigate conversations and embrace the local spirit:

Respectful Interactions:

Politeness is paramount. Use courteous greetings, acknowledgements (like "please" and "thank you"), and respectful titles (Mr., Ms., etc.).

Manners matter. When offering or receiving something, use both hands to show respect.

Beyond Words:

Body language speaks volumes. Maintain eye contact and utilize appropriate gestures to convey your message. Be mindful that gestures can hold different meanings across cultures, so adapt accordingly.

Tech Tools for Travellers:

Embrace translation apps and offline dictionaries. Tools like Google Translate or Microsoft Translator bridge language barriers in real-time, translating text, speech, and even images.

Finding Help:

Tourist Information Centers are your friends. Scattered throughout the city, multilingual staff can provide maps, brochures, and invaluable guidance.

Navigating Accents:

Cantonese reigns supreme, but with regional variations. Be patient, listen attentively, and don't hesitate to ask for clarification if needed.

Respectful Pronunciation:

Learn the Cantonese pronunciations of key places. This is especially helpful for navigating public transportation or asking for directions. Respect local pronunciations and spellings, even if they differ from English.

Cultural Immersion:

Go beyond basic phrases. Language exchange programs or cultural immersion experiences offer deeper connections. Engage in conversations, attend language meetups, or participate in workshops to truly appreciate Hong Kong's rich linguistic and cultural heritage.

The Takeaway:

By respecting local customs, leveraging translation tools, and interacting with locals in a courteous manner, you'll unlock a richer communication experience in Hong Kong. Embrace the opportunity to learn, and delve into the city's captivating tapestry of languages!

CHAPTER THREE

TOP ATTRACTION

Hong Kong's magic unfolds across a tapestry of attractions, catering to every taste. From heart-stopping thrills to serene moments steeped in history, here are 10 experiences that will leave you breathless:

Victoria Peak: A City Unveiled - Ascend to Victoria Peak, the city's crown jewel. Take the historic Peak Tram or conquer the challenging hiking trails, and be rewarded with panoramic vistas of the dazzling Hong Kong skyline, Victoria Harbour, and the outlying islands.

Hong Kong Disneyland: Where Dreams Take Flight - Unleash your inner child at Hong Kong Disneyland. Explore whimsical lands like Adventureland and Fantasyland, meet beloved Disney characters, and experience exhilarating rides that guarantee a day filled with laughter and unforgettable memories.

Ocean Park: A Dive into Adventure - Dive deep into the aquatic wonders of Ocean Park. This sprawling theme park and oceanarium offers something for everyone. Encounter fascinating marine life at the Grand Aquarium, get your adrenaline pumping on thrilling roller coasters, or be captivated by the educational animal shows and interactive exhibits.

Tian Tan Buddha: A Beacon of Serenity - Lantau Island offers a spiritual sanctuary. Here, the majestic Tian Tan Buddha, one of the world's largest seated bronze Buddha statues, exudes tranquility. Surrounded by lush mountains and serene landscapes, this iconic landmark embodies harmony and peace.

Ngong Ping 360: Soaring Above it All - Embark on a breathtaking cable car journey with Ngong Ping 360. Glide above the picturesque landscapes of Lantau Island, marveling at the panoramic views of the mountains, the sparkling sea, and the awe-inspiring Tian Tan Buddha below. Your journey culminates at Ngong Ping Village, a vibrant hub brimming with cultural experiences and entertainment.

Symphony of Lights: A Glittering Spectacle - Witness a nightly masterpiece - the Symphony of Lights. This dazzling multimedia extravaganza illuminates the Hong Kong skyline with a synchronized display of lights, music, and lasers. Watch in awe as iconic buildings along both sides of Victoria Harbour come alive in a mesmerizing dance of light and sound.

Temple Street Night Market: A Sensory Feast - Immerse yourself in the electrifying energy of Temple Street Night Market. Stroll through a maze of bustling stalls overflowing with treasures. Haggle for unique souvenirs and clothing, savor delectable street food, or even have your fortune told. This vibrant market is a quintessential Hong Kong experience.

Man Mo Temple: A Journey Through Time - Step back in time at Man Mo Temple, a historic haven dedicated to the Taoist gods of literature (Man) and war (Mo). Admire the intricate details of the temple's architecture, the exquisite wood carvings, and the fragrant incense that fills the air with a sense of peace and tranquility.

Wong Tai Sin Temple: A Tapestry of Faith - Wong Tai Sin Temple beckons with its vibrant colors and profound spiritual significance. Explore the temple grounds, where worshippers come to pray for blessings and seek guidance from the gods. Be captivated by the energetic atmosphere and the architectural details that showcase the rich Taoist heritage.

Hong Kong Museum of History: Unearthing the Past - Embark on a journey through time at the Hong Kong Museum of History. Interactive exhibits, captivating artifacts, and multimedia presentations bring the city's fascinating past to life. Explore Hong

Kong's evolution from its ancient roots to its modern-day metropolis.

Victoria Peak

Victoria Peak *A Must-See Destination in Hong Kong*

Speaker Notes Victoria Peak, also known simply as The Peak, is a must-visit destination for any traveler to Hong Kong. Towering over the city at 552 meters (1,811 feet), it offers breathtaking panoramic views, lush greenery, and a vibrant atmosphere. This presentation will explore how to get to the Peak, what to do once you arrive, and the best time to visit.

Reaching the Peak

- **Peak Tram:** The most popular and scenic way to reach Victoria Peak.
- **Bus:** Several bus routes service the Peak, including the Peak Tram Bus (No. 15).
- **Taxi/Car:** Offers flexibility but can encounter traffic and limited parking.

Speaker Notes There are three main ways to reach Victoria Peak. The Peak Tram is the most popular option, offering a funicular railway ride with incredible views up the mountain. Buses are a more economical option, while taxis and cars provide the most flexibility but can encounter traffic congestion, especially during peak hours.

Activities and Attractions

- **Sky Terrace 428:** The highest viewing platform offering 360-degree panoramic views.
- **Peak Tower:** A distinctive landmark housing shops, restaurants, and Madame Tussauds Hong Kong.
- **Peak Galleria:** A shopping and dining complex with a rooftop garden and observation deck.
- **Peak Circle Walk:** A scenic hiking trail with panoramic views and historical landmarks.

Speaker Notes Once you reach the summit, there are many exciting things to see and do. The Sky Terrace 428 offers unparalleled 360-degree views of Hong Kong, perfect for capturing stunning photos. The Peak Tower is a must-see for its architecture, shops, restaurants, and the popular Madame Tussauds wax museum. For those seeking some exercise and nature, the Peak Circle Walk provides a scenic trail with breathtaking vistas.

Best Time to Visit

- Clear weather conditions for optimal visibility.
- **Early mornings or evenings:** Avoid crowds and capture stunning sunrises or sunsets.
- **Weekdays:** Generally less crowded than weekends and public holidays.

Speaker Notes Victoria Peak is a popular attraction year-round, but the best time to visit depends on your preferences. For the clearest views, aim for a day with clear skies. Early mornings and evenings offer beautiful sunrises and sunsets, but tend to be more crowded. If you prefer a more relaxed experience, consider visiting on a weekday, as weekends and public holidays can get busy.

Conclusion

- A captivating experience for all visitors.
- Unparalleled views, exciting attractions, and outdoor adventures.
- A must-do on any Hong Kong itinerary.

Hong Kong Disneyland

Hong Kong Disneyland, a captivating realm of fantasy and adventure, awaits on Lantau Island. Steeped in the enchanting world of Disney, this theme park promises unforgettable experiences for guests of all ages. Let's embark on a journey through its wonder:

Themed Lands: A World of Endless Exploration

Main Street, U.S.A.: Step back in time and stroll down charming streets reminiscent of turn-of-the-century America. Delectable treats, delightful shops, and classic Disney melodies fill the air, setting the stage for a day of enchantment.

Fantasyland: Where dreams take flight! Soar through the skies with Peter Pan, embark on a whimsical boat ride through "It's a Small World," or befriend everyone's favorite elephant, Dumbo. Fantasyland brings classic Disney stories to life around every corner.

Adventureland: Channel your inner explorer and delve into thrilling adventures. Navigate the treacherous waters of the Jungle River Cruise, encounter swashbuckling pirates, or unearth hidden treasures in exotic jungles.

Tomorrowland: Blast off to a future filled with high-tech wonders! Pilot a spaceship through the cosmos on Space Mountain, join Buzz Lightyear on an intergalactic battle, or explore the wonders of innovation in this futuristic realm.

Toy Story Land: Shrink down to the size of a toy and join Woody, Buzz, and the gang in this whimsical land inspired by the beloved Pixar films. Hurl through space on RC Racer or experience the thrill of freefall on the Toy Soldier Parachute Drop.

Grizzly Gulch: Saddle up for a rootin' tootin' good time in the Wild West! Explore gold rush-era attractions, savor frontier-themed grub, and conquer the thrilling Big Grizzly Mountain Runaway Mine Cars.

Mystic Point: Unveil the mysteries that lie within this captivating land. Encounter exotic artifacts, delve into the supernatural at Mystic Manor, and explore the wonders of this enchanting realm.

Entertainment and Shows:

Immerse yourself in a world of captivating performances. From dazzling musical productions to delightful character meet-and-greets, Hong Kong Disneyland offers a variety of live entertainment options. Don't miss the awe-inspiring "Disney in the Stars" fireworks show, a nighttime spectacle that paints the sky with dazzling pyrotechnics and beloved Disney music.

Dining and Shopping:

Embark on a culinary adventure! Indulge in a variety of delectable treats, from quick-service snacks to gourmet meals featuring international flavors and Disney-themed delights. Throughout the park, discover shops and boutiques brimming with souvenirs, toys, and Disney merchandise to commemorate your magical visit.

Best Time to Visit:

For a more relaxed experience, consider visiting Hong Kong Disneyland during weekdays or off-peak seasons to avoid crowds and long wait times. Special events, like Halloween and Christmas, transform the park with festive decorations and unique entertainment offerings, making them a delightful time to visit.

Embrace the Magic:

Hong Kong Disneyland is a realm where dreams become reality and imagination knows no bounds. From heart-pounding adventures to heartwarming encounters with beloved characters, this unforgettable destination promises memories that will last a lifetime. So, pack your bags, unleash your inner child, and prepare to be swept away by the magic of Hong Kong Disneyland!

Ocean Park

Ocean Park Hong Kong isn't your average theme park. This sprawling marine-themed wonderland, perched on the southern coast of Hong Kong Island, offers an exhilarating blend of education, entertainment, and conservation. Spanning over 91 hectares, Ocean Park promises an unforgettable journey into the world's oceans and beyond. Let's dive into the exciting zones and experiences that await:

Unveiling the Ocean's Wonders: Marine World

Marine World takes center stage, showcasing the incredible diversity of our oceans. Marvel at the majestic creatures of the Grand Aquarium, come face-to-fin with sharks at Shark Mystique, or witness playful sea lions at Pacific Pier. The Chinese Sturgeon Aquarium offers a glimpse into a critically endangered species.

Thrilling Adventures Await: Thrill Mountain

Calling all adrenaline junkies! **Thrill Mountain** is your playground. Conquer your fears on the heart-stopping Hair Raiser coaster, plummet down The Flash vertical drop ride, or take a spin on the exhilarating Whirly Bird.

Journey to the Poles: Polar Adventure

Polar Adventure transports you to the Earth's coldest regions. Meet adorable penguins, witness playful seals, and come nose-to-nose with arctic foxes. Don't miss the South Pole Spectacular, an immersive exhibit showcasing a replica Antarctic research station.

Unleash Your Inner Explorer: Adventure Land

Get ready for action-packed adventures at **Adventure Land**. Tackle the rushing rapids, navigate the twists and turns of the Mine Train coaster, or brave the soaking fun of the Raging River water ride.

A Celebration of Asian Wildlife: Amazing Asian Animals

Amazing Asian Animals highlights the rich tapestry of wildlife found across Asia. Observe the gentle giants, giant pandas, or witness the fiery red pandas. Swing by to see the golden snub-nosed monkeys and the prehistoric-looking Chinese alligators.

Into the Lush Unknown: Mysterious Rainforest

Mysterious Rainforest beckons with its vibrant flora and fauna. Explore the interactive exhibits teeming with exotic plants and captivating creatures. Immerse yourself in the Rainforest Adventures indoor exhibit or take a scenic ride on the Rainforest Funicular outdoor escalator.

Panoramic Views from Above: Ocean Park Tower

Soar above the excitement and capture breathtaking vistas aboard the **Ocean Park Tower**. This 360-degree observation tower offers panoramic views of the entire park, the surrounding islands, and the vast expanse of the South China Sea.

Shows and Entertainment Galore

Ocean Park isn't just about rides and exhibits! Be captivated by the amazing feats of dolphins at the Ocean Theatre show. Marvel at the playful antics of sea lions and friends in their dedicated show. And as night falls, be dazzled by the Symbio! multimedia extravaganza, featuring a stunning display of lights, water effects, and music.

Protecting Our Oceans: Conservation and Education

Ocean Park goes beyond entertainment. They are a frontrunner in marine conservation and education. The park actively participates in wildlife preservation efforts, research projects, and educational programs designed to inspire visitors to protect our precious oceans.

Delicious Dining and Memorable Shopping

After a thrilling day, treat yourself to a world of culinary delights. From international flavors to local favorites and themed restaurants, Ocean Park offers a variety of dining options to tantalize your taste buds. Commemorate your visit by browsing through the shops and boutiques, picking up souvenirs, gifts, and unique marine-themed merchandise.

The Perfect Time to Visit

To make the most of your Ocean Park adventure, consider weekdays and off-peak seasons for shorter wait times. The park also comes alive during special events and festivals like Halloween and Christmas, offering unique entertainment and themed attractions.

A World of Unforgettable Experiences

Ocean Park Hong Kong is a unique blend of exhilarating adventures, educational experiences, and a commitment to protecting our marine life. Whether you crave aquatic encounters, heart-pounding rides, or captivating shows, Ocean Park offers something for everyone. So, pack your bags, embrace your sense of adventure, and get ready to dive into the magic of Ocean Park Hong Kong!

Tian Tan Buddha

Tian Tan Buddha (The Big Buddha) *A Beacon of Peace and Tranquility in Hong Kong*

Speaker Notes Tian Tan Buddha, also widely known as the Big Buddha, is a majestic bronze statue situated atop Ngong Ping Plateau on Lantau Island, Hong Kong.

Standing at an impressive 34 meters (112 feet) tall, it is one of the world's largest seated outdoor bronze statues. This presentation will explore the history and significance of the Big Buddha, how to get to the site, and what visitors can expect to experience.

History and Construction

- Construction began in 1990 and completed in 1993.
- Part of the Ngong Ping 360 development project.
- Crafted using traditional Buddhist iconography and bronze casting techniques.
- Intricate details and symbolic motifs incorporated into the design.
- Sits on a lotus throne atop a three-tiered pedestal representing enlightenment stages in Buddhism.

Speaker Notes Construction of Tian Tan Buddha commenced in 1990 and was finalized in 1993. The statue's creation coincided with the Ngong Ping 360 development project, which aimed to boost tourism and cultural exchange on Lantau Island. The Big Buddha was meticulously crafted using time-tested bronze casting techniques and incorporates traditional Buddhist symbolism within its design. The intricate details and motifs hold significant meaning, while the lotus throne and three-tiered pedestal upon which the Buddha sits represent the progressive stages of enlightenment in Buddhism.

Significance and Symbolism

- A powerful symbol of peace, harmony, and compassion.
- Represents the connection between humanity and nature.
- A place for spiritual reflection and prayer.
- Visitors come to seek blessings for good health, happiness, and prosperity.

Speaker Notes Tian Tan Buddha holds deep spiritual and cultural significance for Buddhists and visitors alike. The statue embodies the values of peace, harmony, and compassion, while also serving as a powerful symbol of the interconnectedness between humanity and the natural world. Many visitors come to the Big Buddha to pay their respects, offer prayers, and seek blessings for good health, happiness, and prosperity in their lives.

Visiting Tian Tan Buddha

- Ascend 268 steps to reach the base of the statue.
- Enjoy panoramic views of the mountains and Po Lin Monastery.
- Explore Ngong Ping Village with shops, restaurants, and attractions.

Speaker Notes The journey to Tian Tan Buddha involves climbing a flight of 268 steps leading up to the base of the statue. Along the way, pilgrims and tourists can take in the breathtaking panoramic vistas of the surrounding mountains and the nearby Po Lin Monastery. Once you reach the base, you can explore Ngong Ping Village, a vibrant complex featuring shops, restaurants, and various attractions.

Po Lin Monastery

- A revered Buddhist temple founded in 1906.
- Features a collection of Buddhist relics, artifacts, and scriptures.
- Serene meditation halls, prayer rooms, and landscaped gardens.
- Participate in traditional Buddhist rituals, ceremonies, and meditation practices.

Speaker Notes Adjacent to Tian Tan Buddha lies Po Lin Monastery, a revered Buddhist temple established in 1906. The monastery houses a rich collection of Buddhist artifacts, relics, and sacred scriptures, and features tranquil meditation halls, prayer rooms, and beautifully landscaped gardens. Visitors are welcome to participate in traditional Buddhist rituals, ceremonies, and meditation practices, offering an opportunity to immerse themselves in the serenity and spirituality of this sacred place.

Best Time to Visit

- Weekdays and early mornings for fewer crowds.
- Consider visiting during off-peak seasons for a serene experience.

Speaker Notes To maximize your experience at Tian Tan Buddha, consider visiting during weekdays or early mornings to avoid large crowds and long wait times. If you seek a more peaceful and contemplative atmosphere, visiting during off-peak seasons might be the ideal choice.

Conclusion

- A magnificent symbol of Buddhist art, culture, and spirituality.
- Offers a glimpse into Hong Kong's rich heritage and traditions.
- A memorable and enlightening experience for all visitors.

Ngong Ping 360

Speaker Notes Ngong Ping 360 is a must-do experience for visitors to Hong Kong. This scenic cable car ride offers breathtaking panoramic vistas of Lantau Island's natural beauty, traversing over lush landscapes, towering mountains, and the island's dramatic coastline. Spanning approximately 5.7 kilometers, Ngong Ping 360 provides a convenient and unforgettable way to access popular attractions like Tian Tan Buddha, Po Lin Monastery, and Ngong Ping Village. Whether you're seeking adventure, cultural immersion, or simply a chance to marvel at the stunning scenery, Ngong Ping 360 promises a captivating journey into the heart of Lantau Island.

Cable Car Options

- Standard Cabin: Provides expansive views through large glass windows
- Panoramic vistas of mountains, forests, and the South China Sea
- Ideal for sightseeing and photography
- Crystal Cabin: Features a transparent glass bottom for a thrilling experience
- Bird's-eye view of the landscape below
- Perfect for adventurous riders and photography enthusiasts

Speaker Notes Ngong Ping 360 offers two distinct cable car experiences to cater to different preferences. The standard cabin features large glass windows, providing passengers with unobstructed panoramic vistas of the surrounding landscapes. These cabins are ideal for sightseeing and capturing stunning photographs of the lush forests, towering mountains, and the vast expanse of the South China Sea. For a truly unique and exhilarating experience, the crystal cabin boasts a transparent glass bottom. This allows riders to enjoy a bird's-eye view directly below the cable car, creating the sensation of soaring above the breathtaking scenery. The crystal cabin is a perfect choice for adventurous riders and photography enthusiasts seeking a truly unique perspective.

Unforgettable Sights Along the Route

- Tian Tan Buddha (Big Buddha): Witness the majestic Tian Tan Buddha

- One of the world's largest seated outdoor bronze statues
- Located atop Ngong Ping Plateau and surrounded by serenity
- Po Lin Monastery: Discover a tranquil Buddhist sanctuary
- Founded in 1906 and rich in spiritual heritage
- Explore serene courtyards, prayer halls, and meditation gardens
- Ngong Ping Village: Immerse yourself in a vibrant cultural hub
- Diverse shops offering souvenirs, local crafts, and delicious cuisine
- Interactive exhibits showcasing the history and traditions of Lantau Island

Speaker Notes As you soar above the scenic landscapes of Lantau Island on Ngong Ping 360, you'll encounter several must-see attractions along the route. A definite highlight is the majestic Tian Tan Buddha, one of the world's largest seated outdoor bronze statues. Located atop Ngong Ping Plateau, the Tian Tan Buddha exudes an air of serenity and is surrounded by breathtaking mountain vistas. Another captivating stop is Po Lin Monastery, a revered Buddhist temple founded in 1906. Nestled amidst lush greenery, the monastery offers a haven of peace and tranquility, with serene courtyards, prayer halls, and meditation gardens perfect for spiritual reflection. Your journey also includes Ngong Ping Village, a vibrant complex featuring a diverse range of shops, restaurants, and attractions. Here, you can explore traditional architecture, savor delectable local delicacies, and delve into interactive exhibits showcasing the rich history and cultural traditions of Lantau Island.

Tips for an Optimal Experience

- Purchase tickets in advance to avoid long queues, particularly during peak seasons.

Speaker Notes To make the most of your Ngong Ping 360 experience, here are a few helpful tips. Consider purchasing your tickets in advance, especially during peak tourist seasons or holidays. This will help you avoid long queues at the ticket counters and allow you to proceed directly to boarding the cable car.

Choosing Your Cable Car Cabin

- Standard Cabin: Ideal for sightseeing and relaxation
- Provides expansive views through large windows
- Perfect for families and those seeking a comfortable ride
- Crystal Cabin: For

Symphony of Lights

The Symphony of Lights isn't just a show - it's a Hong Kong landmark. This nightly extravaganza, recognized by Guinness World Records, transforms Victoria Harbour into a dazzling canvas of color, music, and light. Get ready to be mesmerized by the synchronized illuminations and captivating energy that defines Hong Kong.

Witness the Magic Unfold

- Every night at 8 PM (Hong Kong time), the city comes alive.

The Symphony of Lights is a free, 10-minute show best enjoyed from the waterfront promenades along Victoria Harbour. Find your perfect spot at:

- Tsim Sha Tsui Promenade: Soak in unobstructed views from the waterfront walkway or relax on a designated seating area.
- Central Promenade: Unwind on the benches and admire the panoramic spectacle of illuminated Central and Admiralty districts.
- Golden Bauhinia Square: Witness the Symphony of Lights against the iconic Golden Bauhinia statue and the Wan Chai skyline.

Want a different perspective? Enjoy the show from a rooftop bar, a cruise on the harbor, or an observation deck offering breathtaking city vistas.

A Multisensory Feast

The Symphony of Lights is more than just mesmerizing visuals. Here's what elevates the experience:

- **Illuminated Cityscapes:** Over 40 buildings lining the harbor participate in the show. Their facades come alive with synchronized patterns, colors, and dazzling effects, creating a captivating display.
- **Music in Harmony:** A specially composed soundtrack perfectly complements the light show. The music's rhythm and style are in sync with the illuminations, creating a truly immersive audiovisual experience.
- **Interactive Elements:** Engage with the Symphony of Lights through mobile apps, social media, and special programs. Share your experience, photos, and videos using designated hashtags and online platforms.

A Celebration of Hong Kong

The Symphony of Lights is more than a show; it's a celebration of Hong Kong's spirit. The vibrant colors, synchronized lights, and uplifting music showcase the city's dynamism, culture, and innovative character.

So, come witness the Symphony of Lights in Hong Kong. Let the dazzling displays and captivating music leave you in awe, capturing the unforgettable essence of this remarkable city.

Symphony of Lights in Hong Kong *A Dazzling Display of City, Music, and Light*

Speaker Notes The Symphony of Lights is more than just a show - it's a Hong Kong landmark. This nightly extravaganza, recognized by Guinness World Records, transforms Victoria Harbour into a dazzling canvas of color, music, and light. Get ready to be mesmerized by the synchronized illuminations and captivating energy that defines Hong Kong.

A Nightly Spectacle Unfolds

Every night at 8 PM (Hong Kong time), the city comes alive with a free, 10-minute light and sound show.

Witness the magic from the waterfront promenades along Victoria Harbour:

Tsim Sha Tsui Promenade: Soak in unobstructed views from the waterfront walkway or relax on a designated seating area.

Central Promenade: Unwind on the benches and admire the panoramic spectacle of illuminated Central and Admiralty districts.

Golden Bauhinia Square: Witness the Symphony of Lights against the iconic Golden Bauhinia statue and the Wan Chai skyline.

Enjoy a different perspective? View the show from a rooftop bar, a cruise on the harbor, or an observation deck offering breathtaking city vistas.

Speaker Notes The Symphony of Lights is a free, nightly show that takes place at 8:00 PM Hong Kong time. The best vantage points are along the promenades of Victoria Harbour. Find your perfect spot at Tsim Sha Tsui Promenade for unobstructed views, relax on the Central Promenade benches, or take in the scene with the Golden Bauhinia statue in the foreground at Golden Bauhinia Square. For a unique experience, consider enjoying the show from a rooftop bar, a harbor cruise, or an observation deck.

A Multisensory Feast for the Senses

The Symphony of Lights is more than just mesmerizing visuals. Here's what elevates the experience:

Illuminated Cityscapes: Over 40 buildings lining the harbor participate in the show. Their facades come alive with synchronized patterns, colors, and dazzling effects, creating a captivating display.

Music in Harmony: A specially composed soundtrack perfectly complements the light show. The music's rhythm and style are in sync with the illuminations, creating a truly immersive audiovisual experience.

Interactive Elements: Engage with the Symphony of Lights through mobile apps, social media, and special programs. Share your experience, photos, and videos using designated hashtags and online platforms.

Speaker Notes The Symphony of Lights is a multisensory feast that goes beyond just visual spectacle. Over 40 buildings along Victoria Harbour come alive with synchronized lighting effects, transforming the cityscape into a dazzling display of color and movement. A specially composed soundtrack complements the visuals, creating a harmonious blend of sight and sound. The show even features interactive elements, allowing you to engage through mobile apps, social media, and special programs. Don't forget to share your experience and photos using designated hashtags!

A Celebration of Hong Kong's Spirit

The Symphony of Lights is more than a show; it's a celebration of Hong Kong's spirit.

The vibrant colors, synchronized lights, and uplifting music showcase the city's dynamism, culture, and innovative character.

The show is enhanced with special effects and themed presentations during festive occasions like Chinese New Year, Christmas, and National Day.

Visitors can enjoy themed versions of the show featuring holiday decorations, seasonal music, and custom-designed lighting displays.

Speaker Notes The Symphony of Lights is more than a show; it's a vibrant celebration of Hong Kong's spirit. The dazzling displays and uplifting music capture the city's dynamism, cultural richness, and innovative character. The show is further enhanced during festive occasions and holidays. Expect special effects, themed presentations, holiday decorations, seasonal music, and custom lighting displays during Chinese New Year, Christmas, and National Day, adding an extra layer of excitement and festivity to the experience.

A History of Illumination

The Symphony of Lights debuted in 2004 to commemorate a special occasion.

Debuting on July 1, 2004, the Symphony of Lights marked the 7th anniversary of the establishment of the Hong Kong Special Administrative Region (HKSAR).

A collaborative

CHAPTER FOUR
CULTURAL EXPERIENCE

Hong Kong isn't just a world-class city with towering skyscrapers. It's a vibrant tapestry of Chinese culture, ancient traditions, and contemporary energy. Get ready to explore temples and tea ceremonies, savor delectable cuisine, and immerse yourself in the sights, sounds, and festivals that define Hong Kong.

Experience the Essence of Chinese Traditions

Festivals and Celebrations: Immerse yourself in the excitement of Chinese New Year parades, marvel at the colorful lanterns of the Mid-Autumn Festival, or witness the traditions of various celebrations throughout the year.

Temples and Shrines: Discover architectural marvels like Man Mo Temple and Wong Tai Sin Temple. Explore these sacred sites and observe traditional rituals that connect you to Hong Kong's religious heritage.

Embrace Wellness and Ancient Practices

Tai Chi in the Park: Join a Tai Chi class or witness practitioners performing their routines along the waterfront. This graceful form of martial arts promotes physical and mental well-being, offering a glimpse into a holistic approach to health.

The Art of Tea Appreciation: Delve into the meditative world of tea ceremonies at traditional tea houses. Learn about tea-making techniques, sample various teas, and savor the cultural significance of this ancient tradition.

Explore the Work of Skilled Artisans

Traditional Crafts and Workshops: Discover the intricate techniques of calligraphy, pottery, silk weaving, and paper cutting from skilled artisans. Witness the preservation of time-honored crafts and support the local art scene.

Unveil the Magic of Cantonese Opera

A Cultural Spectacle: Witness the captivating performances of Cantonese opera. Experience elaborate costumes, stylized movements, and melodious music at venues like the Xiqu Centre. Immerse yourself in this unique and vibrant art form.

Embark on a Culinary Adventure

A World of Flavors: Explore Hong Kong's diverse culinary scene. Sample traditional Cantonese delicacies, savor street food delights, and discover regional specialties from around China. Indulge in a delicious journey through Hong Kong's rich food culture.

Uncover Hong Kong's History

Heritage Trails and Museums: Trace the city's fascinating evolution from a fishing village to a global metropolis. Explore historic neighborhoods and museums like the Hong Kong Museum of History, and delve into the stories that shaped this dynamic city.

Immerse Yourself in a Cultural Extravaganza

Festivals and Performances: Hong Kong's cultural calendar is brimming with exciting events. Attend art exhibitions, witness music festivals, or enjoy dance performances. Immerse yourself in the city's vibrant arts scene and discover local and international talent.

Wander Through Bustling Streets

Traditional Markets and Street Scenes: Explore the lively energy of Hong Kong's street markets. Navigate through the Temple Street Night Market, Ladies' Market, or Sham Shui Po, and experience the sights, sounds, and smells that capture the essence of the city's unique street culture.

Embrace the Spirit of Hong Kong

Hong Kong offers a captivating blend of tradition and innovation. From ancient temples to contemporary art scenes, and from street food stalls to Michelin-starred restaurants, the city invites you to explore its cultural tapestry. So come, discover the heart of Hong Kong, and embark on an unforgettable journey through Asia's world city.

Temple Street Night Market

The Temple Street Night Market isn't just a market - it's a pulsating kaleidoscope of sights, sounds, and flavors that captures the essence of Hong Kong's vibrant nightlife. Nestled in Yau Ma Tei, Kowloon, this open-air market explodes with life in the evenings, transforming Temple Street and its surrounding alleys into a shopper's paradise, a foodie's haven, and an entertainer's playground.

Shop 'Til You Drop (or Until You Score a Deal!)

Temple Street Night Market is a bargain hunter's dream. Rows upon rows of stalls overflow with an eclectic mix of merchandise: clothing, accessories, electronics, souvenirs, and even antiques. Haggling with vendors is part of the experience, so put your negotiating skills to the test and unearth unique treasures at unbeatable prices.

A Culinary Adventure for Daring Palates

Foodies, rejoice! Temple Street Night Market is a smorgasbord of culinary delights. From iconic Hong Kong bites like fish balls and egg waffles to adventurous treats like stinky tofu, the market caters to all appetites. Indulge in regional specialties like curry fish balls and grilled squid, or savor comforting clay pot rice. Don't be afraid to step outside your comfort zone - the aroma of sizzling dishes and the vibrant energy of the food stalls will surely tempt you.

Live Entertainment Under the Neon Glow

Temple Street Night Market isn't just about shopping and eating. It's a stage for captivating performances. Witness street performers showcase their talents, be mesmerized by magic shows, or catch a glimpse of traditional Cantonese opera. The energy is infectious, with live music and impromptu acts adding to the market's already vibrant atmosphere.

A Glimpse into Local Culture

Temple Street Night Market is a portal to Hong Kong's soul. Immerse yourself in the local culture as you navigate the bustling crowds, marvel at the colorful signage, and lose yourself in the symphony of sounds.

People-watch, capture the neon-lit chaos in photographs, and soak up the infectious energy that defines Hong Kong's nightlife.

Unwind and Explore After Dark

The Temple Street Night Market typically comes alive in the late afternoon and thrives well into the night. The peak hours unfold after sunset, offering you ample time to shop, savor delicious food, and enjoy the entertainment until late.

An Unforgettable Hong Kong Experience

A visit to Temple Street Night Market is a must for anyone seeking a taste of authentic Hong Kong. It's a sensory explosion, a cultural immersion, and a guaranteed exciting evening filled with discoveries around every corner. So come, explore the stalls, indulge in the street food, and be captivated by the vibrant energy of this one-of-a-kind night market.

Man Mo Temple

Man Mo Temple isn't just a historic landmark - it's a portal to Hong Kong's soul. Nestled in Sheung Wan district, this Taoist temple, built in 1847, is a captivating blend of ornate architecture, spiritual significance, and cultural heritage. Dedicated to Man Cheong, the god of literature, and Kwan Tai, the god of war, Man Mo Temple offers a glimpse into the city's rich traditions and timeless beliefs.

A Tapestry of Design and Devotion

Step into Man Mo Temple and be greeted by the grandeur of traditional Chinese architecture. The temple's facade boasts a striking red and gold color scheme, while its roof ridges and intricate wood carvings depict mythical creatures and deities. Inside, the central hall features a mesmerizing display of incense coils hanging from the ceiling. Altars dedicated to Man Cheong and Kwan Tai stand adorned, while murals showcase scenes from Chinese mythology, transporting you to a world of legend and folklore.

A Haven for Spiritual Seekers

Man Mo Temple is a haven for worshippers seeking blessings and guidance. Offerings of incense, fruit, and flowers are presented to the deities as acts of reverence. Whether seeking success in studies, career advancement, or protection from harm, Man Mo Temple serves as a sanctuary for those seeking spiritual solace and divine intervention.

A Legacy That Endures

As one of Hong Kong's oldest temples, Man Mo Temple embodies the city's cultural heritage. It's a testament to the enduring influence of Chinese religion and philosophy. The temple's serene atmosphere and traditional rituals offer visitors a window into the spiritual practices and beliefs that have shaped Hong Kong's past and present.

Immerse Yourself in the Experience

Explore the temple's halls and courtyards, marvel at its architectural details, and witness worshippers paying homage to the deities. The temple's tranquil ambiance provides a welcome respite from the city's vibrancy, allowing you to find a moment of peace and reflection.

Celebrating Traditions Throughout the Year

Man Mo Temple comes alive throughout the year with cultural events and festivals. Witness Taoist rituals, traditional ceremonies, and vibrant celebrations during Lunar New Year and Mid-Autumn Festival. These events offer a chance to experience the temple's energetic atmosphere and participate in age-old customs.

Conveniently Located for Exploration

Man Mo Temple is easily accessible, situated in the heart of Sheung Wan. A short walk from the Sheung Wan MTR station, the temple's central location makes it a perfect stop while exploring the surrounding markets, neighborhoods, and attractions.

A Journey Beyond the Walls

Man Mo Temple's story extends beyond its physical structure. Delve deeper and discover its rich history:

1847: Constructed during the Qing Dynasty by community leaders seeking a place of worship.

Dedicated Deities: Man Cheong (literature) and Kwan Tai (war & righteousness) reflect the diverse beliefs of Hong Kong's community.

Witnessing Ceremonies and Rituals

Observe traditional Taoist ceremonies performed by priests and worshippers.

Witness the burning of incense, chanting of prayers, and offerings presented to the deities. The main hall becomes the focal point for these practices.

A Legacy to Preserve

Man Mo Temple's cultural significance is recognized. It's classified as a Grade I historic building, ensuring its preservation for future generations.

A Source of Inspiration

The temple's beauty and mystique have captivated filmmakers, writers, and artists. Its image has been featured in numerous films and literary works.

A Community Hub

Man Mo Temple remains active, hosting events, festivals, and educational programs for the community and visitors. It serves as a gathering space, fostering a sense of belonging.

Local Legends and Allure

Stories of benevolent spirits and guardian deities surround the temple, adding to its mystique and charm.

A Timeless Symbol

Man Mo Temple is more than a structure; it's a symbol of Hong Kong's cultural heritage and spiritual legacy. Visit Man Mo Temple and embark on a journey through history, belief, and the enduring spirit of this remarkable city.

Wong Tai Sin Temple

Speaker Notes Wong Tai Sin Temple is a revered Taoist temple located in the Kowloon district of Hong Kong. It's a popular destination for worshippers seeking blessings, guidance, and divine intervention. The temple is renowned for its vibrant atmosphere, intricate architecture, and cultural significance, making it a must-visit destination for tourists and locals alike.

History and Legend

- Founded in 1921 to honor Wong Tai Sin, a legendary Taoist deity.
- Legend says Wong Tai Sin was a 4th-century monk known for healing powers, supernatural abilities, and benevolence.

- Devotees believe prayers to Wong Tai Sin bring miracles and fulfill wishes, especially in health, prosperity, and love.

Speaker Notes Wong Tai Sin Temple was founded in 1921 to honor the legendary Taoist immortal Wong Tai Sin, also known as Huang Chu-ping. According to legend, Wong Tai Sin was a 4th-century Taoist monk renowned for his healing powers, supernatural abilities, and benevolent spirit. Devotees believe that prayers offered to Wong Tai Sin can bring about miracles and fulfill wishes, particularly in matters of health, prosperity, and love.

Architecture and Design

- Blend of traditional Chinese architectural styles
- Iconic vermilion pillars, golden roofs, and ornate carvings
- Main hall dedicated to Wong Tai Sin with a sacred statue
- Other halls for various Taoist deities like the Three Pure Ones and the Eight Immortals

Speaker Notes Wong Tai Sin Temple features a blend of traditional Chinese architectural styles, with its iconic vermilion pillars, golden roofs, and ornate carvings adorning its halls and pavilions. The temple's main hall, dedicated to Wong Tai Sin, houses a sacred statue of the deity surrounded by offerings of incense, flowers, and fruits. Other halls and altars within the temple complex are dedicated to various Taoist deities, including the Three Pure Ones and the Eight Immortals.

Cultural Significance

- Center of Taoist worship and spiritual practice
- Millions of visitors annually, including worshippers, pilgrims, and tourists
- Renowned for fortune-telling services by Taoist priests and fortune-tellers

Speaker Notes Wong Tai Sin Temple holds significant cultural importance as a center of Taoist worship and spiritual practice in Hong Kong. It attracts millions of visitors each year, including worshippers, pilgrims, and tourists seeking blessings and guidance from the deity. The temple is also renowned for its fortune-telling services, where visitors can consult Taoist priests and fortune-tellers for insights into their future, relationships, and career prospects.

Visitor Experience

- Explore intricately decorated halls, pavilions, and courtyards
- Admire architecture, sculptures, and religious artifacts
- Participate in traditional rituals and practices
- Light incense, make offerings, and pray for blessings

Speaker Notes Visitors to Wong Tai Sin Temple can explore its intricately decorated halls, pavilions, and courtyards, admiring the architecture, sculptures, and religious artifacts on display. Many visitors participate in traditional rituals and practices, such as lighting incense, making offerings, and praying for blessings at the main altar of Wong Tai Sin.

Festivals and Events

- Variety of cultural events and festivals throughout the year
- Taoist rituals, religious ceremonies, and festive celebrations
- Most popular event: Wong Tai Sin Birthday Celebration on lunar new year's 8th day
- Temple adorned with lanterns, decorations, and performances

Speaker Notes Wong Tai Sin Temple hosts a variety of cultural events and festivals throughout the year, including Taoist rituals, religious ceremonies, and festive celebrations. One of the most popular events is the Wong Tai Sin Birthday Celebration, held annually on the eighth day of the lunar new year. During this festival, the temple is adorned with lanterns, decorations, and performances, attracting thousands of devotees and tourists.

Surrounding Area

- Vibrant neighborhood with bustling markets, shops, and eateries
- Explore Good Wish Garden, a tranquil oasis with greenery and ponds

- Sample local delicacies at nearby food stalls and restaurants

Chi Lin Nunnery

Imagine stepping into a world of serene beauty. Nestled amidst the verdant hills of Diamond Hill in Kowloon lies Chi Lin Nunnery, a haven of Buddhist tranquility. Here, meticulously crafted wooden structures, tranquil gardens, and ornate Buddhist relics whisper tales of ancient traditions and spiritual enlightenment.

A Journey Through Time

Chi Lin Nunnery's roots stretch back to the Tang Dynasty (618-907 AD), a golden age of Buddhist art and culture in China. Originally a refuge for nuns seeking spiritual wisdom, the nunnery has flourished into a revered center of Buddhist learning and practice. Its name, "Chi Lin," evokes the mythical unicorn, a symbol of purity, virtue, and auspiciousness in Chinese folklore.

Architectural Grandeur

Step through the gates and be captivated by the architectural marvels. Traditional Chinese design principles come alive in elegant symmetry, graceful curves, and intricate woodwork. Interconnected halls, pavilions, and courtyards adorned with ornate carvings, colorful murals, and gilded decorations form the heart of the nunnery. Each structure, meticulously crafted using time-honored techniques, embodies the timeless beauty of Chinese craftsmanship.

A Communion with Nature

Beyond the main complex lies a haven of tranquility - meticulously landscaped gardens, ponds, and rockeries designed to evoke harmony and balance. Meander along serene paths, admire the lotus ponds reflecting the sky, and find solace amidst bonsai trees and manicured shrubs. These gardens are an invitation to connect with nature, fostering meditation, reflection, and spiritual contemplation.

Treasures Unveiled

Within the halls and chambers of Chi Lin Nunnery lies a treasure trove of Buddhist artifacts, scriptures, and relics, each imbued with spiritual significance and historical importance. Exquisite statues of Buddha and Bodhisattvas, intricately carved sutra scrolls, and ceremonial objects adorned with precious metals and intricate designs showcase the rich tapestry of Buddhist art, culture, and philosophy.

A Living Tapestry of Faith

Chi Lin Nunnery is more than just a museum; it's a living monastery. Here, Buddhist nuns dedicate themselves to a life of prayer, meditation, and compassionate service. Witness daily rituals and ceremonies, from chanting and prostrations to offering incense, and experience the transformative power of Buddhist practice firsthand. The nunnery also offers meditation classes, Dharma talks, and retreats for those seeking deeper understanding of Buddhist teachings.

Reaching Outward

Chi Lin Nunnery extends its influence beyond its walls. Educational programs, cultural events, and social welfare initiatives foster connections with the local community. Collaborations with schools, universities, and organizations promote Buddhist values of compassion, wisdom, and social harmony. Through outreach, Chi Lin Nunnery inspires individuals of all backgrounds to cultivate inner peace, engage in interfaith dialogue, and contribute to the well-being of society.

A Lasting Sanctuary

Chi Lin Nunnery, a timeless beacon of Buddhist spirituality, architectural beauty, and cultural heritage, welcomes all. Whether seeking solace, enlightenment, or a respite from the urban buzz, a visit here promises a sacred journey. As you wander through its hallowed halls, inhale the calming fragrance of incense, and gaze upon serene landscapes, may you find peace, inspiration, and a renewed connection to the wisdom within.

Ten Thousand Buddhas Monastery

High atop a verdant hill in Hong Kong's Sha Tin, the Ten Thousand Buddhas Monastery beckons. This sanctuary isn't just a place; it's a journey - a transformative ascent towards enlightenment. Prepare to be enveloped by serenity as you climb a path lined with thousands of golden Buddhas, each radiating tranquility and guiding you on your quest for inner peace.

A Legacy of Faith

Though named for the multitude of Buddhas adorning its halls, the Ten Thousand Buddhas Monastery isn't a traditional monastery but a Taoist temple complex. Founded in the 1950s by Reverend Yuet Kai, a devout Buddhist monk, it's renowned for its grandeur, ornate decorations, and sacred relics. The name signifies the countless Buddhas here, each embodying a unique path to enlightenment and compassion.

The Climb to Tranquility

Your pilgrimage begins with a symbolic ascent. As you conquer the 431 steps, you're greeted by countless arhats - enlightened disciples - lining the path. Each step is a metaphor, a challenge overcome on the road to spiritual awakening. With each golden Buddha you encounter, a sense of serenity washes over you, urging you onward.

A Tapestry of Majesty

Reaching the summit, you're met with a breathtaking spectacle. The Ten Thousand Buddhas Monastery unfolds before you – a majestic complex of halls, pagodas, and pavilions adorned with intricate carvings, vibrant murals, and a symphony of colors. The main hall houses a magnificent Buddha Shakyamuni statue, flanked by rows of golden Buddhas, bodhisattvas, and celestial beings. Here, the past and present intertwine in a harmonious blend of traditional Chinese and modern architectural influences.

A Sanctuary for the Soul

Within the monastery's serene courtyards and gardens, find solace for your soul. Whether you choose to sit silently under ancient trees or join a guided meditation led by resident monks, the tranquility here fosters introspection and spiritual renewal. The calming atmosphere invites you to connect with the deeper truths of existence, offering a refuge from the outside world's chaos.

Treasures Beyond Measure

The Ten Thousand Buddhas Monastery is a treasure trove of cultural significance. Explore its exhibition halls and galleries, where centuries-old scriptures, artifacts, and relics whisper tales of the past. Among the most revered is a relic of the Buddha's tooth, imbued with the power of healing and protection.

Reaching Outward

The monastery extends its wisdom beyond its walls. Through educational programs, cultural events, and charitable initiatives, it actively engages with the community. Workshops, lectures, and retreats offer people of all backgrounds the opportunity to explore Buddhist philosophy, meditation, and the path to mindfulness. The Ten Thousand Buddhas Monastery strives to promote harmony, understanding, and spiritual awakening in our ever-changing world.

A Journey Within

The Ten Thousand Buddhas Monastery is more than a destination; it's a transformative experience. Whether you seek enlightenment, inspiration, or simply a moment of peace, this sacred sanctuary offers a journey within. As you walk among the golden Buddhas, breathe in the fragrant incense, and feel the serenity embrace you, may you discover wisdom, inner peace, and a renewed connection to the boundless spirit within.

Hong Kong Museum of History

Step into a captivating journey through time at the Hong Kong Museum of History, nestled in the heart of Kowloon's Tsim Sha Tsui district. This museum isn't just a collection of artifacts; it's a portal to Hong Kong's vibrant cultural heritage, from the whispers of ancient civilizations to the pulse of modern life. Whether you're a history buff or simply curious, the museum promises an enriching experience for all.

A Walk Through Time

The museum unfolds like a captivating story. Explore thematic galleries that chronicle Hong Kong's evolution, from prehistoric settlements to the dynamism of the present day. Each gallery delves into key periods, events, and figures that shaped the city's character. Interactive exhibits, multimedia presentations, and life-like dioramas bring history to life, allowing you to witness the past firsthand.

Treasures Unearthed

Venture beyond the timelines and discover the museum's prized possessions. An extensive collection of artifacts awaits, whispering tales of bygone eras. From bronze age tools and ceramic pottery to colonial-era memorabilia and contemporary artworks, each piece offers a glimpse into the lives of Hong Kong's diverse population. Marvel at a replica of a traditional Chinese junk boat, or lose yourself in immersive recreations of historical streets and vibrant neighborhoods.

A Tapestry of Cultures

Hong Kong's identity thrives on its rich multicultural tapestry. The museum celebrates this vibrant mix through its exhibits, highlighting the contributions of various ethnicities, religions, and communities. Explore the influence of Chinese festivals and traditions, delve into the remnants of British colonial rule, and discover how global trends have interwoven with the city's cultural fabric. This nuanced portrayal fosters a deeper appreciation for Hong Kong's remarkable diversity.

Igniting Curiosity

The Hong Kong Museum of History isn't just about showcasing the past; it's about igniting curiosity for all ages. Beyond its permanent exhibitions, the museum offers a plethora of educational programs, workshops, and guided tours designed to deepen your understanding. Interactive exhibits, hands-on activities, and multimedia presentations make learning engaging and fun, perfect for families, students, and anyone with a thirst for knowledge.

A Community Hub

The museum extends its reach beyond its walls, actively engaging with the local community. Through outreach programs, partnerships with schools and universities, and collaborative initiatives with cultural organizations, the museum fosters a sense of ownership and pride in the city's heritage. Special events, lectures, and cultural festivals celebrate Hong Kong's unique identity and spark conversations that bridge cultures. By empowering individuals to become stewards of their cultural legacy, the museum paves the way for a more positive and inclusive future.

A Lasting Impression

The Hong Kong Museum of History transcends the role of a museum; it's a vibrant cultural hub. Whether you're exploring its galleries, participating in interactive programs, or engaging with the community events, a visit here promises a lasting impression. Let the museum be your guide as you unveil the rich tapestry of Hong Kong's history, heritage, and the ever-evolving cultural spirit that defines this remarkable city.

CHAPTER FIVE

OUTDOOR ADVENTURE

Hong Kong pulsates with urban energy, but beyond the neon lights and towering skyscrapers lies a world of natural wonders waiting to be explored. From rugged mountain trails to idyllic island getaways, Hong Kong offers a diverse outdoor playground for adventurers of all stripes.

Step into Nature's Embrace

Lace up your hiking boots and conquer the iconic Dragon's Back trail, with its panoramic views of the South China Sea. For a more challenging trek, venture into the New Territories and scale the peaks, each offering a unique perspective on Hong Kong's beauty.

Island Hopping Adventure

Set sail on an island adventure. Kayak through the clear waters surrounding Lamma Island, or explore the stilted houses and fishing villages of Tai O. Each island boasts its own charm, from bustling markets to secluded beaches, promising an unforgettable escape.

Rock Climbing Challenge

Calling all adrenaline seekers! Hong Kong's granite cliffs and rocky outcrops provide the perfect terrain for rock climbing and bouldering. Test your skills on challenging routes at Lion Rock or savor the breathtaking city views from atop Beacon Hill. Whether you're a seasoned climber or a curious beginner, Hong Kong's welcoming community offers opportunities for everyone.

Embrace the Water

Hong Kong's coastline beckons water enthusiasts. Catch some waves at Big Wave Bay, try your hand at paddleboarding, or explore the underwater world through scuba diving or snorkeling excursions. Discover vibrant coral reefs teeming with marine life, a hidden treasure beneath the waves.

Explore on Two Wheels

Hit the open road and explore Hong Kong on a cycling adventure. Cruise along scenic waterfront promenades or challenge yourself on mountain bike trails that weave through verdant country parks. Whether you prefer leisurely rides or adrenaline-pumping adventures, Hong Kong's diverse cycling routes cater to all levels.

A Sanctuary Amidst the City

Escape the urban buzz and find solace in Hong Kong's network of nature reserves and country parks. Hike through the lush forests of Tai Mo Shan Country Park, spot diverse birdlife in the Mai Po Nature Reserve, or simply soak in the tranquility of nature's embrace. These protected areas offer a haven for wildlife and a chance to reconnect with the earth.

An Unforgettable Escape

Hong Kong is more than just a bustling metropolis. It's a land of hidden trails, pristine islands, and thrilling adventures. From mountain peaks to hidden coves, Hong Kong's natural beauty offers endless possibilities for exploration, discovery, and rejuvenation. So, trade the concrete jungle for the thrill of the outdoors and embark on an unforgettable adventure in Hong Kong.

Lantau Island and Ngong Ping Village

Lantau Island isn't just Hong Kong's biggest island; it's an adventurer's paradise. Lush greenery, pristine beaches, and a rich cultural tapestry await those seeking escape from the urban buzz. Here, amidst the natural beauty, lies Ngong Ping Village, a vibrant hub and gateway to the island's most captivating experiences.

Trek Through Untamed Beauty

Lace up your boots and explore Lantau Island's extensive network of hiking trails. Weave through rugged terrain, marvel at breathtaking vistas, and encounter the island's diverse wildlife. The Lantau Trail, a 70-kilometer odyssey, beckons those seeking a multi-day adventure. For shorter jaunts, conquer Sunset Peak, follow the contemplative Wisdom Path, or explore the Ngong Ping Nature Trail. Each path unveils a unique perspective on Lantau Island's magic.

Soar Above the Scenery

Embark on a thrilling journey aboard the Ngong Ping 360 cable car. This 25-minute adventure whisks you over lush landscapes, dramatic coastlines, and the vast South China Sea. As you glide in your comfortable cabin, capture panoramic vistas, spot playful dolphins, and create memories that will last a lifetime.

Immerse Yourself in Culture

Ngong Ping Village welcomes you with a vibrant embrace of Hong Kong's heritage. Explore traditional tea houses, discover local crafts at artisan workshops, and find unique souvenirs to treasure back home. Ascend to Ngong Ping Plateau and stand in awe before the Tian Tan Buddha, one of the world's largest outdoor bronze statues, radiating serenity amidst the mountains.

Find Inner Peace

Neighboring Ngong Ping Village, the historic Po Lin Monastery beckons. Delve into its ornate architecture, tranquil gardens, and sacred relics, gaining insights into Hong Kong's Buddhist traditions. Explore the monastery's halls and prayer areas, marveling at intricate carvings and ancient artifacts. Nearby, the Wisdom Path offers a serene retreat. Walk along its wooden columns inscribed with verses from the Heart Sutra, a revered Buddhist scripture, and find a moment of peace amidst the natural beauty.

Embrace the Thrill

The adventures extend beyond Ngong Ping Village. Explore Tai O, a traditional fishing village on stilts, with guided eco-tours. Kayak or paddleboard along the island's scenic coastline, or take a boat trip to hidden coves. For water enthusiasts, beaches offer opportunities for windsurfing and other exciting activities. Nature lovers can delve into Lantau Island's lush forests and protected nature reserves, where serenity and discovery intertwine.

A Land of Timeless Memories

Lantau Island and Ngong Ping Village offer an unforgettable escape. Hike scenic trails, soar above breathtaking landscapes, and immerse yourself in cultural wonders. Whether you seek heart-pounding adventures or tranquil retreats, Lantau Island promises a treasure trove of experiences. So, pack your spirit of exploration and embark on a journey to discover the natural beauty and cultural richness that lie at the heart of Hong Kong.

Dragon's Back Hike

The Dragon's Back isn't just a trail; it's a Hong Kong legend. Nestled on Hong Kong Island's southeastern coast, this exhilarating hike promises stunning scenery, diverse wildlife, and a challenging climb that will test your limits and leave you breathless in the best way possible.

A Trail of Enchanting Vistas

The 5.3-kilometer Dragon's Back winds along the spine of Shek O Country Park, aptly named for its resemblance to a dragon's scales. As you ascend, lush forests and grassy slopes give way to panoramic coastal vistas. The turquoise waters stretch towards the horizon, while the iconic Hong Kong skyline paints the distance. Take a moment to capture breathtaking photos or simply soak in the serene beauty.

A Haven for Nature Lovers

The Dragon's Back isn't just visually stunning; it's a haven for nature enthusiasts. Hike amidst a diverse tapestry of flora and fauna. Spot indigenous trees, vibrant flowers, and flitting butterflies. Keep your eyes peeled for native birds like bulbuls and sunbirds, or for the rare treat of a Hong Kong paradise flycatcher or elusive Chinese pangolin.

A Challenge Worth Conquering

While suitable for all levels, the Dragon's Back demands moderate fitness. Steep inclines, uneven steps, and exposed sections can be challenging, especially in hot weather. But don't let that deter you! The reward of breathtaking views and the thrill of conquest make the effort worthwhile. Push your limits, embrace the adventure, and celebrate your accomplishment at the summit.

Traces of the Past

The Dragon's Back whispers tales of the past. Along the trail, remnants of ancient stone walls, abandoned villages, and traditional farming terraces offer glimpses into Hong Kong's rural history and indigenous communities. Interpretive signs unveil the area's geology, ecology, and cultural heritage, enriching your understanding of this special place.

An Unforgettable Escape

The Dragon's Back Hike is more than just a trek; it's an unforgettable escape. It's a chance to challenge yourself, connect with nature, and discover the hidden beauty of Hong Kong Island. So lace up your boots, grab your camera, and embark on a legendary adventure that will leave you wanting to explore more. The Dragon's Back awaits.

Sai Kung Peninsula and Geopark

Escape the urban jungle and delve into the wild beauty of Sai Kung Peninsula and Geopark. Nestled in Hong Kong's northeastern corner, Sai Kung offers a haven for outdoor enthusiasts, with rugged coastlines, pristine beaches, and a treasure trove of natural wonders waiting to be explored.

A Geological Wonderland

Embark on a geological odyssey at the UNESCO-listed Sai Kung Geopark. Dramatic rock formations, sea caves, and volcanic landscapes paint a picture of the Earth's history. Hike along the High Island Geo Trail or the Sharp Island East Nature Trail and marvel at hexagonal volcanic columns, sea arches, and ancient rock formations. Sai Kung's geological marvels are a testament to the powerful forces that shaped our planet.

Water Playground Awaits

Sai Kung's pristine coastline beckons water adventurers. Kayak through hidden coves, explore offshore islands teeming with marine life on a snorkeling trip, or simply cruise along on a boat tour. The crystal-clear waters provide the perfect backdrop for a refreshing escape. Unwind on the sandy shores of Sai Kung's many islands, like Sharp Island, Kiu Tsui Chau, and Yim Tin Tsai. Swim, sunbathe, or picnic under the warm sun – the choice is yours.

Hiking Adventures for Every Trekker

Lace up your boots and explore Sai Kung's diverse landscapes on a network of well-maintained hiking trails. Whether you're a seasoned hiker or a casual explorer, there's a trail for you. The Sai Kung East Country Park boasts challenging routes like the MacLehose Trail and the Wilson Trail, offering scenic vistas and breathtaking encounters with nature. For those seeking an adrenaline rush, the Sai Kung Volcanic Rock Region promises rugged terrain, steep ascents, and panoramic rewards.

A Journey Through Time and Culture

Sai Kung's rich cultural heritage intertwines with its natural beauty. Explore traditional fishing villages like Tai O and Sai Kung Town, where time seems to stand still. Witness ancient customs, crafts, and traditions that have been passed down for generations. Historical landmarks like the Tin Hau Temple and the Old Quarrymen's Village offer glimpses into the region's maritime past and indigenous culture. Immerse yourself in the unique cultural tapestry that makes Sai Kung special.

Protecting Paradise

Sai Kung Peninsula and Geopark are dedicated to preserving this natural and cultural wonder for future generations. Environmental education programs, guided eco-tours, and community initiatives promote responsible tourism practices. By fostering a sense of stewardship, Sai Kung ensures its natural beauty remains pristine.

An Unforgettable Escape

Sai Kung Peninsula and Geopark offer more than just an escape; they offer an experience. Hike dramatic landscapes, paddle through clear waters, or explore ancient villages. Whether you seek adventure or tranquility, Sai Kung promises an unforgettable encounter with nature and culture. So, pack your bags, embrace the spirit of exploration, and discover the wonders of Sai Kung Peninsula and Geopark.

Hong Kong Park

Hong Kong pulsates with energy, but a haven of tranquility awaits amidst the towering skyscrapers. Hong Kong Park, an urban oasis, offers a surprising escape for nature lovers, fitness enthusiasts, and families seeking outdoor recreation.

A Tapestry of Gardens

Immerse yourself in a world of botanical wonders. Explore themed gardens like the serene Tai Chi Garden or the vibrant Forsgate Conservatory, bursting with exotic orchids and tropical blooms. Spot native birds fluttering in the Edward Youde Aviary, or find a quiet corner for meditation by the tranquil ponds of the Central Garden.

Urban Adventure Awaits

Hong Kong Park isn't just about strolling. Jogging trails weave through the park, while fitness stations and outdoor gyms offer opportunities to get your heart pumping. Challenge friends to a game at the Sports Centre, or let loose with the kids at the Children's Playground, featuring slides, climbing structures, and interactive fun.

Culture and History

Step back in time at the Flagstaff House Museum of Tea Ware. Explore its collection of antique teapots and artifacts, offering a glimpse into the rich history of Chinese tea culture. The Edward Youde Memorial Pavilion, a traditional Chinese structure, provides a picturesque backdrop for cultural events and ceremonies.

Learning Through Nature

Hong Kong Park isn't just a playground; it's a classroom. The Environmental Education Centre offers interactive exhibits and workshops, fostering awareness of conservation and green living. Participate in educational programs and discover the importance of protecting our planet's biodiversity.

A Breath of Fresh Air in the City

Hong Kong Park is more than just a park; it's an urban sanctuary. Escape the city's clamor and reconnect with nature. Explore verdant gardens, challenge yourself with outdoor activities, or delve into local culture. With its diverse attractions and vibrant atmosphere, Hong Kong

Park beckons you to embrace the spirit of exploration and tranquility, all within the heart of Hong Kong.

Tai O Fishing Village

Far from the neon glow of Hong Kong, Tai O Fishing Village whispers tales of the sea. Nestled on Lantau Island's western coast, Tai O offers a glimpse into a bygone era, where stilt houses hug the water and life revolves around the rhythm of the tides. Here, outdoor enthusiasts can explore a captivating blend of natural beauty, cultural heritage, and unforgettable adventures.

Explore by Boat: Where Dolphins Dance

Unveil Tai O's magic from a unique perspective – a boat. Weave through scenic waterways, past iconic stilt houses, and out to open water. Keep your eyes peeled for playful pods of Chinese white dolphins – a breathtaking encounter in their natural habitat! Capture unforgettable moments as these majestic creatures frolic in the waves.

Hiking Trails: Unveiling Nature's Wonders

Beyond the village, a network of trails beckons. Embark on an adventure through lush mangrove forests, coastal wetlands, and rugged hillsides. Discover hidden waterfalls, scenic viewpoints, and diverse ecosystems teeming with life. Popular routes like the Tai O Infinity Pool Trail and the Tai O Family Trail offer diverse experiences, each a testament to Tai O's natural splendor.

A Step Back in Time: Immersing in Culture

Tai O's soul lies in its rich heritage. Wander narrow alleyways lined with traditional stilt houses, temples, and bustling seafood markets. Breathe in the salty air and soak up the sights, sounds, and energy of this vibrant fishing community. Delve deeper at the Tai O Heritage Hotel. Guided tours and workshops unveil the village's history, architecture, and maritime traditions, offering a window into the heart of Tai O's cultural tapestry.

A Feast for the Senses: Savoring Local Delights

No Tai O adventure is complete without indulging in its culinary treasures. Freshly caught seafood, prepared with generations-old recipes, awaits. Savor grilled fish, slurp down shrimp paste noodles, or tantalize your taste buds with local salted fish specialties – all enjoyed at waterfront restaurants overlooking the charming harbor. For an authentic experience, visit the bustling seafood markets. Purchase the day's catch and local delicacies to enjoy at home or on a scenic picnic by the sea.

Preserving Paradise: A Sustainable Future

Tai O embraces sustainable practices to protect its natural beauty and cultural heritage. Community initiatives, guided eco-tours, and educational programs raise awareness about marine conservation, mangrove preservation, and responsible fishing practices. By promoting eco-tourism and environmental stewardship, Tai O ensures its coastal ecosystems and cultural traditions remain a wonder for generations to come.

A Timeless Escape: The Call of the Coast

Tai O Fishing Village beckons with its unique charm. Explore its waterways, hike through its wild landscapes, or savor its seafood delights. Immerse yourself in a timeless world where tradition thrives and the rhythm of the tide sets the pace. Let Tai O whisk you away on an unforgettable coastal adventure, where Hong Kong's rich fishing heritage comes alive.

CHAPTER SIX

CULINARY DELIGHTS

Hong Kong's culinary scene is as diverse and vibrant as its skyline, offering a tantalizing array of flavors, aromas, and culinary traditions from around the world. From traditional Cantonese cuisine to international fusion dishes, Hong Kong's food culture reflects its rich history, cultural diversity, and cosmopolitan flair. Whether you're exploring bustling street markets, elegant fine dining establishments, or hidden local eateries, Hong Kong promises a gastronomic adventure that will tantalize your taste buds and leave you craving for more.

Dim Sum:

No visit to Hong Kong is complete without indulging in the city's iconic dim sum, bite-sized delights that are synonymous with Cantonese cuisine. Dim sum, which translates to "touch the heart," encompasses a variety of savory and sweet dumplings, buns, and small dishes that are typically served with tea. From steamed shrimp dumplings (har gow) and barbecue pork buns (char siu bao) to custard tarts (dan tat) and rice noodle rolls (cheung fun), dim sum offers a delightful culinary experience that is best enjoyed with friends and family in a traditional tea house or dim sum restaurant.

Roast Meats:

Hong Kong is renowned for its succulent roast meats, which are often showcased in restaurant windows and street-side stalls, enticing passersby with their tantalizing aromas and crispy skin. Roast duck, roast goose, and roast pork are among the most popular choices, each prepared using traditional Cantonese cooking techniques and served with a side of fragrant rice or noodles. Whether you're dining at a Michelin-starred restaurant or a local eatery, Hong Kong's roast meats are sure to satisfy your cravings for savory, mouthwatering flavors.

Seafood:

With its proximity to the sea, Hong Kong boasts a bounty of fresh seafood that is celebrated in its local cuisine. Visitors can feast on a variety of seafood delicacies, including steamed fish, stir-fried clams, and braised abalone, at seafood restaurants and dai pai dongs (open-air food stalls) throughout the city. For a truly immersive experience, head to Aberdeen Floating Village or Sai Kung Fishing Village, where you can dine on freshly caught seafood while overlooking the scenic harbor and bustling waterfront.

Street Food:

Hong Kong's vibrant street food scene offers a cornucopia of flavors and aromas that tantalize the senses and satisfy cravings on the go. From savory snacks like egg waffles (gai daan jai) and fish balls (yu dan) to sweet treats like mango sticky rice and egg tarts, street food vendors offer a diverse array of culinary delights that cater to every palate and budget. Whether you're exploring the bustling streets of Mong Kok, Temple Street Night Market, or the bustling alleys of Central, Hong Kong's street food stalls promise a delicious culinary adventure that's as authentic as it is affordable.

International Cuisine:

In addition to its traditional Cantonese fare, Hong Kong is a melting pot of international flavors and cuisines, reflecting its status as a global city with a diverse population. Visitors can savor a wide range of international dishes, including Japanese sushi, Korean barbecue, Indian curry, and Italian pasta, at restaurants, cafes, and food courts throughout the city. Whether you're craving exotic flavors or familiar comforts, Hong Kong's international dining scene offers something for every taste and preference, making it a culinary destination that caters to the appetites of food lovers from around the world.

Conclusion:

Hong Kong's culinary delights offer a feast for the senses and a journey of discovery through the flavors, aromas, and culinary traditions of the city's diverse cultures and communities. Whether you're indulging in traditional dim sum, savoring succulent roast meats, or exploring the vibrant street food scene, Hong Kong promises a gastronomic adventure that will leave you craving for more. So come hungry, leave satisfied, and embark on a culinary journey through the vibrant streets and savory delights of Hong Kong.

Dim Sum restaurants

Looking for an unforgettable dim sum experience in Hong Kong? Look no further! This list highlights some of the city's best restaurants, offering everything from Michelin-starred delights to hidden local gems.

1. Tim Ho Wan (添好運): Affordable Michelin-Starred Dim Sum

Tim Ho Wan wears the crown as the "world's cheapest Michelin-starred restaurant." Here, you'll find authentic dim sum at wallet-friendly prices. Don't miss their legendary baked BBQ pork buns, har gow (steamed shrimp dumplings), and pan-fried lo bak go (turnip cakes). Multiple locations across Hong Kong ensure convenience, making Tim Ho Wan a favorite for both locals and visitors.

2. Lin Heung Tea House (蓮香樓): A Step Back in Time

Established in 1926, Lin Heung Tea House is a dim sum institution. Experience a traditional atmosphere with bustling energy and classic decor. Savor a variety of dim sum classics like steamed pork ribs, lotus leaf-wrapped sticky rice, and egg custard tarts, all served from bamboo steamers. Embrace the lively experience with roaming trolleys, communal tables, and the buzz of conversation.

3. DimDimSum Dim Sum Specialty Store (點點心點心專門店): Modern Takes on Dim Sum Favorites

Craving a modern twist on dim sum? DimDimSum offers a contemporary setting for enjoying innovative creations alongside traditional favorites. Indulge in truffle and mushroom dumplings, lava custard buns, and crispy spring rolls bursting with shrimp and cheese. The restaurant's cozy ambiance and friendly service make it perfect for dim sum enthusiasts of all ages, with multiple locations conveniently spread across Hong Kong.

4. Maxim's Palace City Hall (美心皇宮): Grand Dim Sum with a View

Located in Central's City Hall, Maxim's Palace City Hall is a grand destination for dim sum. Opulent decor, panoramic harbor views, and an extensive menu await you. Choose from classic dim sum dishes like steamed dumplings, BBQ pork buns, and rice noodle rolls, all served in a traditional banquet setting. Arrive early, as this popular spot tends to get crowded during peak hours.

5. One Dim Sum (一點心): A Hidden Gem for High-Quality Dim Sum

Venture into the Prince Edward neighborhood to discover One Dim Sum, a local favorite known for its high-quality dim sum at reasonable prices. Their menu boasts a delightful variety of traditional and innovative dishes, including steamed shrimp dumplings, pan-fried turnip cakes, and baked egg custard tarts. The unassuming exterior gives way to a cozy interior, offering a warm and welcoming ambience for dim sum lovers.

6. Din Tai Fung (鼎泰豐): World-Renowned Dumpling Delights

Hailing from Taiwan, Din Tai Fung has become a world-renowned name for dumplings and dim sum delicacies. Their Hong Kong branches serve up delectable steamed dumplings, featuring their signature xiao long bao (soup dumplings), alongside other classic dim sum dishes like steamed buns, wontons, and fried rice cakes. Expect an elegant ambiance and attentive service, making Din Tai Fung a refined choice for dim sum aficionados.

Street food favorites

Hong Kong's streets are a haven for foodies, bursting with vibrant flavors and unique textures. From sweet treats to savory delights, here's a taste of the city's most iconic street food finds:

Egg Waffles (Gai Daan Jai): A Textural Delight

These golden gems aren't just for breakfast. Made with sweet batter and cooked in a special iron, egg waffles boast a crispy exterior and fluffy interior. Enjoy them plain or explore creative flavors like chocolate, green tea, or even savory options.

Fish Balls (Yu Dan): A Bite-Sized Treat on the Go

A Hong Kong classic, fish balls are springy spheres of minced fish perfection. Boiled or deep-fried, they're typically served on skewers or in bowls and dunked in flavorful sauces like curry or sweet and sour, making for a satisfying snack.

Curry Fish Balls (Ga Lei Yu Dan): A Spicy Kick

Take your fish ball experience up a notch with curry fish balls. Skewered fish balls are simmered in a fragrant and slightly spicy curry sauce, offering a delightful explosion of taste in every bite. Perfect for a quick pick-me-up while exploring the city.

Stinky Tofu (Chou Dou Fu): For the Adventurous Eater

Don't let the name deter you! Stinky tofu is a must-try for adventurous foodies. Fermented tofu is deep-fried for a crispy exterior and a soft, creamy inside. Served with a tangy dipping sauce, it's a unique and flavorful experience.

Cheung Fun (Rice Noodle Rolls): A Customizable Delight

Cheung fun are steamed sheets of rice noodle rolled with a variety of fillings like shrimp, barbecue pork, or fried dough sticks. Drizzled with sweet or spicy sauces, they're a versatile option for a light snack or a filling meal.

Siu Mai (Shumai): A Savory Bite

Siu mai are bite-sized bundles of deliciousness. Minced pork, shrimp, and mushrooms are encased in a delicate wonton wrapper and steamed to perfection. Enjoy them on their own or with a touch of soy sauce or chili oil for an extra kick.

Egg Tarts (Dan Tat): A Sweet Tradition

These flaky pastries are a quintessential Hong Kong treat. Featuring a buttery crust filled with creamy egg custard, they're the perfect way to satisfy your sweet tooth. Found everywhere from bakeries to street stalls, they're a delightful snack or dessert.

Hong Kong-Style French Toast (Cha Chaan Teng Faan Chai): A Sweet and Savory Twist

This unique take on French toast features thick-cut bread dipped in egg batter, deep-fried golden brown, and then stuffed with peanut butter or sweetened condensed milk. The sweet and savory combination is a surefire crowd-pleaser.

So, venture out, explore the vibrant streets, and discover the culinary magic of Hong Kong's street food scene. Each bite offers a delicious adventure into the city's rich food culture and heritage.

Michelin-starred dining experiences

Hong Kong boasts a dazzling array of Michelin-starred restaurants, each offering an unforgettable epicurean adventure. From innovative twists on Chinese classics to the epitome of French haute cuisine, prepare to be tantalized by culinary artistry.

Bo Innovation: X-treme Chinese Cuisine

Embark on a culinary odyssey at Bo Innovation, where Chef Alvin Leung's "X-treme Chinese" creations redefine Chinese cuisine. Expect unexpected flavor combinations and innovative techniques that push the boundaries of tradition. (Location: Shop 13, 2/F, J Residence, 60 Johnston Road, Wan Chai)

L'Atelier de Joël Robuchon: Interactive French Dining

Witness the magic firsthand at L'Atelier de Joël Robuchon. This acclaimed restaurant features an open kitchen concept, allowing you to observe the mastery of Chef Joël Robuchon's team as they craft exquisite

French dishes with a contemporary twist. (Location: Shop 315 & 401, The Landmark, Central)

Sushi Shikon: Intimate Edomae Experience

For a truly intimate dining experience, look no further than Sushi Shikon. With only a handful of seats, this haven for sushi aficionados offers the opportunity to savor the finest seasonal ingredients, expertly prepared by Chef Yoshiharu Kakinuma in the time-honored Edomae style. (Location: 7/F, 8 Queen's Road Central, Central)

Tate Dining Room: Asian-Infused French Cuisine

Embark on a fusion adventure at Tate Dining Room. Chef Vicky Lau's creations seamlessly blend French techniques with Asian flavors and seasonal ingredients, resulting in stunning presentations that delight both the eyes and the palate. (Location: 210 Hollywood Road, Sheung Wan)

Épure: Refined Contemporary French Cuisine

Treat yourself to a sophisticated dining experience at Épure. Executive Chef Nicolas Boutin curates a menu of elegant French dishes, meticulously crafted with the finest ingredients sourced globally. (Location: Shop 403, 4/F, Ocean Centre, Harbour City, Tsim Sha Tsui)

T'ang Court: The Pinnacle of Cantonese Fine Dining

Indulge in the epitome of Cantonese cuisine at T'ang Court. Renowned for its meticulous attention to detail and unwavering commitment to excellence, this three-Michelin-starred establishment promises a culinary journey defined by classic flavors, impeccable presentation, and exceptional service. (Location: 1/F, The Langham, Hong Kong, 8 Peking Road, Tsim Sha Tsui)

Forum Restaurant: Luxurious Cantonese Delights

Revel in luxury at Forum Restaurant. This Michelin-starred haven offers an exquisite Cantonese dining experience, featuring meticulously prepared dishes showcasing the finest ingredients. (Location: Shop 1103, 11/F, Times Square, 1 Matheson Street, Causeway Bay)

Caprice: French Haute Cuisine at its Finest

Caprice is a celebration of French gastronomy. Chef Guillaume Galliot crafts seasonal masterpieces using innovative techniques, while the elegant ambiance and impeccable service ensure an unforgettable dining experience. (Location: 6/F, Four Seasons Hotel Hong Kong, 8 Finance Street, Central)

Traditional Cantonese cuisine

Hong Kong's culinary scene is a tapestry woven with vibrant flavors, and Cantonese cuisine forms its very foundation. Dive into this rich tradition with these classic dishes, each offering a taste of history and heritage.

Roast Goose (Siu Ngo): A Crispy Delight

Savor the quintessential roast goose (siu ngo), renowned for its glistening, crisp skin and succulent meat. Traditionally roasted with aromatic spices and herbs, this dish is a must-try for any food enthusiast.

Dim Sum: A Culinary Journey in Miniature

Dim sum, meaning "touch the heart," is an experience in itself. Bite-sized delights like steamed dumplings, har gow, and buns filled with savory or sweet ingredients are perfect for sharing and exploring the vast canvas of Cantonese cuisine.

Sweet and Sour Pork (咕嚕肉): A Flavorful Symphony

A beloved comfort food, sweet and sour pork features tender chunks of pork stir-fried with colorful bell peppers, onions, and pineapple. The sweet and tangy sauce creates a symphony of flavors that pairs perfectly with steamed rice.

Unveiling the Ocean's Bounty: Stir-Fried Seafood

Hong Kong's vibrant seafood scene shines through in stir-fried seafood dishes. Fresh shrimp, squid, scallops, and fish are stir-fried with a variety of sauces and seasonings, showcasing the ocean's bounty in every bite.

Steamed Fish: Simplicity that Captivates

Elegance meets simplicity in steamed fish. This dish highlights the delicate flavor and freshness of the fish, typically served whole and seasoned with ginger, scallions, and soy sauce. A healthy and delightful option for any occasion.

Braised Abalone: A Luxurious Indulgence

Abalone, a prized ingredient, takes center stage in braised abalone with oyster sauce. The dish presents a luxurious combination of the abalone's tender texture and rich flavor, elevated by the savory oyster sauce.

Cantonese-Style Congee: Comfort in a Bowl

Warm your soul with Cantonese-style congee. This comforting and nourishing dish is made with long-grain rice simmered into a creamy consistency. Choose from a variety of toppings like preserved egg, shredded chicken, or century egg for a personalized touch.

Wonton Noodle Soup: A Beloved Classic

Wonton noodle soup is a cornerstone of Cantonese cuisine. Savory broth cradles tender wontons filled with shrimp or pork, while springy egg noodles complete this comforting and delicious dish.

Tea culture in Hong Kong

Hong Kong boasts a thriving tea culture, evident in its numerous tea houses. These tranquil havens offer a vast selection of teas, from classic oolong and pu-erh to fragrant blends and herbal infusions. Dim sum and light snacks often grace the menu, making tea houses ideal for socializing and unwinding.

Yum Cha, meaning "drink tea" in Cantonese, is a cherished culinary tradition. Families and friends gather to enjoy dim sum alongside fragrant tea. Steamed dumplings, buns, and rolls are just a few of the bite-sized delights offered during Yum Cha. This social ritual fosters connection and camaraderie.

Tea appreciation is deeply woven into Hong Kong's tea culture. Aficionados relish exploring the subtleties of different tea varietals, brewing methods, and serving styles. Tea appreciation events and workshops pepper the city, offering insights into the history, production, and tasting techniques of various teas. From traditional ceremonies to modern tastings, these events provide a gateway to the rich world of Chinese tea culture.

While tea houses cater to tea enthusiasts seeking serenity, Cha Chaan Tengs offer a more casual atmosphere. These bustling eateries serve comfort food and beverages, including the beloved Hong Kong staple, milk tea. Made with strong black tea and evaporated or condensed milk, milk tea is a must-try. Cha Chaan Tengs are popular for breakfast, lunch, and dinner, where patrons can savor a cup of milk tea alongside classic dishes like pineapple bun with butter, scrambled eggs with toast, and Hong Kong-style noodles.

For those seeking to take a piece of Hong Kong's tea culture home, tea ware shops abound. They offer a diverse selection of teapots, cups, and accessories crafted from porcelain, clay, and other materials. Loose-leaf and packaged teas are also available, allowing visitors to explore the world of Chinese tea and create their own tea-drinking rituals.

Hong Kong's vibrant tea scene flourishes throughout the year with tea festivals, exhibitions, and events. These celebrations showcase the art of tea making, brewing, and appreciation through demonstrations, workshops, and tastings. From the Hong Kong International Tea Fair to the annual Tea Ware Expo, tea lovers have numerous opportunities to immerse themselves in the world of tea and deepen their appreciation for this ancient beverage.

So, embark on a journey through time-honored traditions and modern innovations. Explore the rich tea culture of Hong Kong, a delightful experience for locals and visitors alike.

CHAPTER SEVEN

PRACTICAL INFORMATION

Here's a quick guide to navigating your trip to Hong Kong, from currency exchange to cultural etiquette.

Money Matters:

Currency: Hong Kong uses the Hong Kong Dollar (HKD). Credit cards are widely accepted, but carry cash for smaller vendors.

Communication:

Languages: Cantonese and English are the official languages. Signage and announcements are often bilingual for easy navigation.

Getting Around:

Transportation: Hong Kong boasts a superb public transport system including MTR (subway), buses, trams, ferries, and taxis. Invest in an Octopus Card for convenient fare payment.

Climate:

Weather: Expect hot, humid summers and mild winters. Typhoon season is from May to November, with peak risk between July and September.

Plugging In:

Voltage: Hong Kong uses 220 volts AC, 50Hz. Pack a universal adapter if your devices have different plugs.

Safety First:

Safety: Hong Kong is generally safe, but stay vigilant in crowded areas. Be mindful of belongings and avoid pickpockets.

Healthcare:

Medical Care: Hong Kong offers high-quality healthcare. Dial 999 for emergencies. Consider travel insurance for unexpected medical costs.

Visa Information:

Visa Requirements: Visa needs vary by nationality. Check Hong Kong's visa requirements before your trip.

Time Difference:

Time Zone: Hong Kong operates on Hong Kong Time (HKT), UTC+8, which is 8 hours ahead of Coordinated Universal Time (UTC).

Cultural Cues:

Etiquette: Respect local customs. Dress modestly at temples and avoid public displays of affection. Tipping is not customary, except in upscale restaurants with a service charge.

Transportation options (MTR, buses, trams)

Hong Kong boasts a robust public transport system, making it easy to explore every corner of the city. Here's a breakdown of your options:

MTR (Mass Transit Railway): The MTR is the heart of Hong Kong's network, offering swift, reliable travel across Hong Kong Island, Kowloon, and the New Territories. With over 90 stations, it connects you to major attractions, shopping districts, and residential areas. Trains run from dawn to late night, ensuring convenient journeys in air-conditioned comfort. The Airport Express line whisks you straight to Hong Kong International Airport.

Buses: Complementing the MTR is the extensive bus network. Red minibuses provide a budget-friendly way to explore neighborhoods not covered by the MTR. Double-decker buses and air-conditioned coaches connect major districts, with clear routes and schedules displayed at stops.

Trams: Take a nostalgic ride on the iconic trams, known as "ding dings." Exclusive to Hong Kong Island, they offer a leisurely way to explore Central, Wan Chai, and Causeway Bay. These single-track trams run frequently and boast affordable fares, making them a favorite among locals and tourists.

Ferries: Explore Hong Kong's scenic waterways by ferry. The Star Ferry, a must-do for tourists, ferries you between Central and Tsim Sha Tsui, offering stunning Victoria Harbour views. Ferries also connect to outlying islands like Lantau, Cheung Chau, and Lamma, providing a relaxing escape from the city.

Taxis: Red taxis serve urban areas, while green taxis cover the New Territories and blue taxis operate solely on Lantau Island. Metered and air-conditioned, they're a convenient option for door-to-door travel, especially in areas with limited public transport.

Octopus Card: Your key to hassle-free travel! This rechargeable smart card lets you pay for fares on all public transport options. It can also be used at convenience stores, supermarkets, and vending machines, making it a versatile tool for travelers.

Hong Kong's public transport system is efficient and comprehensive, allowing you to explore the city's vibrant culture, historical sites, and stunning landscapes with ease. So ditch the car and navigate like a local!

Airport transfers

Hong Kong International Airport (HKIA) offers a variety of options to whisk you into the city or vice versa. Here's how to get your trip off to a stress-free start:

Airport Express Train: The speed demon of transfers, the Airport Express zooms between HKIA and downtown Hong Kong. Trains depart every 10 minutes, reaching key destinations like Kowloon and Central in under 30 minutes. Pay with single journey tickets or your Octopus Card.

Airport Shuttle Bus: Headed straight to your hotel? Airport shuttle buses provide door-to-door service across the city. Several companies operate from the Arrival Hall, catering to various destinations and budgets. Check routes, schedules, and fares beforehand.

Taxis: Reliable red taxis await at designated stands. These metered fares include tolls and luggage charges. Travel times depend on your destination and traffic. Green taxis serve the New Territories, and blue taxis operate solely on Lantau Island.

Limousine Service: Arrive in style with a limousine or private car service. Pre-arrange these VIP options through hotels, travel agencies, or private car companies, and enjoy a luxurious welcome to Hong Kong.

Hotel Shuttles: Many hotels offer complimentary shuttle buses to and from HKIA for guests. These operate regularly, providing a convenient option for those staying near major transport hubs. Confirm schedules and availability with your hotel.

Private Transfers: Need ultimate flexibility? Arrange private transfers like cars, vans, or minibuses. Book through travel agencies, online platforms, or directly with transportation companies. These services cater to various group sizes and luggage requirements.

Recommended accommodations (hotels, hostels, guesthouses)

Hong Kong caters to all types of travelers, offering a variety of accommodation options to suit every taste and budget. Here's a guide to help you find the perfect place to stay:

Luxury Hotels:

The Peninsula Hong Kong: For timeless elegance and impeccable service, look no further than The Peninsula Hong Kong. This legendary hotel, located in the heart of Tsim Sha Tsui, boasts stunning views of Victoria Harbour, Michelin-starred restaurants, and luxurious rooms .

Four Seasons Hotel Hong Kong: Immerse yourself in luxury at the Four Seasons Hotel Hong Kong. Situated on Victoria Harbour in Central, this five-star hotel offers panoramic harbor views, world-class amenities, and award-winning dining experiences .

The Ritz-Carlton, Hong Kong: Soar above the city skyline at The Ritz-Carlton, Hong Kong. This iconic hotel, located atop the International Commerce Centre in West Kowloon, offers unparalleled city views, luxurious accommodations, and Michelin-starred restaurants .

Boutique Hotels:

The Pottinger Hong Kong: Experience charm and character at The Pottinger Hong Kong. Nestled in the historic Central district, this boutique hotel offers stylish rooms, personalized service, and easy access to dining and shopping attractions .

Hotel Stage: Embrace contemporary design at Hotel Stage. Located in Jordan, this hotel is known for its sleek design, comfortable rooms, and eco-friendly initiatives, making it a popular choice among modern travelers .

TUVE: Find tranquility amidst the urban buzz at TUVE. This minimalist boutique hotel in Tin Hau is renowned for its Scandinavian-inspired design and attention to detail, providing a serene retreat .

Budget Accommodations:

YesInn: YesInn offers a network of affordable hostel accommodations across Hong Kong. Choose from clean and comfortable dormitory beds, private rooms, and communal facilities - ideal for budget-conscious travelers .

Urban Pack: Enjoy a vibrant atmosphere at Urban Pack. Situated in Tsim Sha Tsui, this hostel provides budget-friendly accommodations with modern amenities and convenient access to shopping, dining, and attractions .

Check Inn HK: Check Inn HK offers cozy rooms and a central location in the lively neighborhood of Tsim Sha Tsui. This guesthouse is a great choice for budget travelers seeking friendly staff and easy access to public transportation .

Serviced Apartments:

The Bauhinia Hotel - Central: Enjoy a convenient home-away-from-home experience at The Bauhinia Hotel. Located in the heart of Central, this hotel offers spacious and well-appointed serviced apartments, perfect for long-stay guests and business travelers .

Citadines Ashley Hong Kong: Citadines Ashley Hong Kong provides contemporary serviced apartments with fully equipped kitchens, modern amenities, and flexible stay options. Situated in Tsim Sha Tsui, this is a great choice for travelers seeking comfort and convenience .

Oakwood Premier AMTD Hong Kong: Indulge in luxurious comfort at Oakwood Premier AMTD Hong Kong. Located in the bustling district of Wan Chai, this property features stylish serviced apartments with state-of-the-art facilities and personalized services for discerning guests .

Currency and banking

Hong Kong uses the Hong Kong Dollar (HKD) as its currency. It's divided into 100 cents, with denominations available in coins (10, 20, 50 cents, $1, $2, $5) and banknotes ($10, $20, $50, $100, $500, $1000).

Exchanging Currency:

Numerous options exist for currency exchange, including airports, banks, hotels, kiosks, and licensed money changers. Popular currencies like USD, EUR, GBP, and JPY are readily exchanged.

Compare rates and fees beforehand to get the best deal. Avoid unlicensed services to prevent scams or counterfeit notes.

Banking Services:

Hong Kong boasts a well-developed banking system with local and international institutions offering various services like accounts, currency exchange, loans, cards, and investments.

Branches and ATMs are widespread, with ATMs often accepting international cards and offering multilingual instructions.

Credit Cards:

Major credit cards like Visa, Mastercard, American Express, and UnionPay are widely accepted, particularly in hotels, restaurants, shops, and attractions.

Carrying some cash is still recommended for smaller purchases and vendors that might not accept cards.

ATMs:

ATMs are readily available throughout the city, located at banks, malls, transport hubs, and tourist areas. Many offer English and other languages for easy cash withdrawals and transactions.

Banking Hours:

Banks typically operate Monday to Friday from 9:00 AM to 4:30 PM. Some may have extended Saturday hours, and specific branches in malls or commercial areas might offer longer hours or even operate on Sundays.

Safety and Security:

Hong Kong is generally safe for banking, but be cautious when using ATMs. Avoid secluded or poorly lit locations. Shield the keypad while entering your PIN and report suspicious activity or unauthorized transactions immediately.

Safety tips and emergency contacts

Hong Kong is a safe city, but a little vigilance goes a long way. Here are some tips to keep you secure:

Personal Safety: Be aware of your surroundings, especially in crowds. Keep valuables close and avoid displaying large sums of cash. Be mindful of traffic and use designated crosswalks.

Health and Hygiene: Practice good hygiene, like washing hands frequently and using sanitizer. Drink bottled or boiled water, and be cautious with street food. Consider travel insurance for medical emergencies.

Emergency Contacts:

Police (emergencies): 999

Fire and Ambulance (emergencies): 999

Consulate (for your home country's assistance): Find contact information beforehand. Keep copies of your passport and travel documents safe.

Natural Disasters: Typhoons are common between May and November. Stay informed about weather forecasts and follow any advisories. Seek shelter if necessary.

Public Transportation Safety: Hold handrails on escalators and walkways. Follow operator rules and respect other passengers. Avoid rushing or pushing, and give up seats to those who need them.

Scams and Fraud Awareness:

Be wary of unsolicited help, especially in tourist areas. These individuals might scam or overcharge you.

Don't share personal or financial information with strangers, especially online or over the phone. Be cautious of suspicious messages or requests for sensitive details.

Report any suspicious activity or scams to the authorities or seek help from your hotel/embassy.

Emergency Preparedness:

Learn evacuation procedures at your hotel and public spaces. Locate fire escapes and emergency exits. Note emergency contact information and evacuation plans displayed in buildings.

Keep valuables like ID, travel documents, medications, and emergency supplies secure and easily accessible. Consider a portable phone charger and flashlight for power outages.

Stay informed about local news, especially during protests or unrest. Avoid areas with demonstrations and follow safety guidelines from local authorities.

Cultural Sensitivity:

Respect local customs and traditions when interacting with residents or visiting religious sites. Dress modestly when entering temples or places of worship, and remove shoes if required.

Be mindful of cultural sensitivities regarding photography. Ask permission before taking photos of people, especially in private settings.

Learn a few basic Cantonese phrases like greetings or polite expressions to show respect for the local language and culture.

CHAPTER EIGHT

SHOPPING AND ENTERTAINMENT

Hong Kong is a shopper's paradise, offering a wide range of options from luxury malls to bustling street markets. Here's a guide to some of the must-visit shopping and entertainment districts:

Shopping Districts:

Causeway Bay: Known for its bustling streets and vibrant atmosphere, Causeway Bay is home to an array of shopping malls, department stores, and boutique shops. Explore Times Square , SOGO Department Store , and Fashion Walk for fashion, electronics, and lifestyle products.

Central: The heart of Hong Kong's financial district, Central offers upscale shopping experiences at luxury boutiques, designer labels, and international brands. Discover The Landmark , IFC Mall , and Pedder Building for high-end fashion and luxury goods.

Tsim Sha Tsui: Located on the Kowloon Peninsula, Tsim Sha Tsui is a shopping paradise with a mix of luxury malls, street markets, and specialty stores. Visit Harbour City , K11 Musea , and Nathan Road for fashion, electronics, and souvenirs.

Street Markets:

Ladies' Market: Dive into the bustling atmosphere of Mong Kok's Ladies' Market, where you'll find bargain-priced clothing, accessories, electronics, and souvenirs . Explore rows of stalls selling everything from fashion items and handbags to toys and trinkets.

Temple Street Night Market: Experience the energy of Temple Street Night Market, a vibrant street market in Jordan known for its lively atmosphere and eclectic mix of stalls . Browse for antiques, electronics, clothing, and street food while soaking in the local culture.

Luxury Shopping:

The Galleria by DFS: Indulge in luxury shopping at The Galleria by DFS, located in Tsim Sha Tsui and Causeway Bay. Discover a curated selection of international luxury brands, fashion, beauty products, and accessories, with duty-free shopping privileges for travelers .

Pacific Place: Immerse yourself in luxury at Pacific Place, an upscale shopping destination in Admiralty featuring designer boutiques, gourmet dining, and lifestyle brands . Explore flagship stores from top fashion houses and enjoy exclusive shopping experiences.

Entertainment Venues:

Hong Kong Disneyland: Embark on a magical adventure at Hong Kong Disneyland, where you can meet beloved Disney characters, experience thrilling rides and attractions, and enjoy spectacular parades and fireworks shows .

Ocean Park: Dive into excitement at Ocean Park, a marine-themed amusement park offering thrilling rides, animal exhibits, and live shows . Explore themed zones like Aqua City, Thrill Mountain, and Polar Adventure for a day of family fun.

Victoria Peak: Take a ride on the Peak Tram to Victoria Peak, the highest point on Hong Kong Island, for breathtaking views of the city skyline and Victoria Harbour . Enjoy shopping, dining, and entertainment options at Peak Galleria and Peak Tower.

Cultural Performances:

Hong Kong Cultural Centre: Experience world-class performances at the Hong Kong Cultural Centre, a renowned venue for music, dance, theater, and opera . Catch performances by the Hong Kong Philharmonic Orchestra, Hong Kong Ballet, and other local and international artists.

Avenue of Stars: Stroll along the Avenue of Stars on the Tsim Sha Tsui waterfront and catch live performances, street buskers, and cultural events against the backdrop of Victoria Harbour . Enjoy stunning views of the skyline and nightly Symphony of Lights show.

Causeway Bay shopping district

Causeway Bay is a shopper's paradise, bursting with malls, department stores, boutiques, and street markets. Here's a peek at what awaits you:

Times Square: This mega-mall boasts over 230 shops across 16 floors. Find fashion, beauty, electronics, and lifestyle brands alongside a food court and cinema .

SOGO Department Store: A must-visit for fashionistas, SOGO offers a vast selection of fashion, cosmetics, homeware, and more across various floors, with designer labels and international brands .

Fashion Walk: Hit the streets of Fashion Walk for trendy finds! Explore the latest fashion trends, streetwear, and accessories at local and international stores .

Lee Gardens: Upscale shopping awaits at Lee Gardens. Find luxury brands, designer boutiques, and gourmet dining spread across Lee Garden One to Six .

Island Beverly Centre: This labyrinthine complex is a haven for fashion adventurers. Discover unique clothing, accessories, and lifestyle products at trendy boutiques .

Hysan Place: Modern design meets curated shopping at Hysan Place. Explore fashion, beauty, and lifestyle brands, and unwind at the rooftop garden with city views .

Street Markets: Don't miss the vibrant street markets! Jardine's Crescent and Fashion Walk Market offer bargain-priced clothing, accessories, and souvenirs.

Mong Kok markets

Mong Kok's markets are a must-visit for any Hong Kong explorer. Get ready for a kaleidoscope of sights, sounds, and incredible finds:

Ladies' Market: Your one-stop shop for bargains! Ladies' Market boasts a massive array of clothing, accessories, gadgets, and souvenirs at budget-friendly prices . Haggling is encouraged, so put your bargaining skills to the test!

Sneaker Street (Fa Yuen Street): Calling all sneakerheads! Fa Yuen Street, aka Sneaker Street, is your haven for athletic shoes, sneakers, and sportswear. Find popular brands, independent retailers, and the latest trends .

Goldfish Street (Tung Choi Street North): Unleash your inner child at Goldfish Street! Explore pet shops and aquarium stores brimming with tropical fish, exotic pets, and pet supplies. It's a feast for the eyes! .

Flower Market Road: Breathe in the sweet fragrance at Flower Market Road. This floral paradise offers a vibrant display of fresh flowers, plants, and gardening supplies. From roses and orchids to bonsai trees, there's something for everyone .

Bird Garden: Escape the urban buzz at the Yuen Po Street Bird Garden. This charming spot is where bird enthusiasts gather to admire and trade songbirds. Listen to the melodious chirping and soak in the tranquil atmosphere .

Mong Kok Computer Centre: Calling all techies! Mong Kok Computer Centre is your one-stop shop for electronics, gadgets, and accessories. Explore floors packed with smartphones, laptops, cameras, and more. Find the latest trends or hidden gems .

Luxury shopping in Central

Central Hong Kong transforms into a shopper's paradise for those seeking the ultimate in luxury retail therapy. Here's a peek at what awaits:

The Landmark: This iconic destination houses an impressive array of high-end fashion boutiques, designer labels, and luxury brands . From renowned fashion houses to exquisite jewelry, prepare to be dazzled by unparalleled selection and exclusive experiences.

IFC Mall (International Finance Centre): Soar to new heights of luxury at IFC Mall. Explore a curated collection of designer boutiques, flagship stores, and lifestyle brands, all nestled within the iconic

International Finance Centre complex . Breathtaking views of Victoria Harbour and the city skyline add to the unforgettable ambience.

The Galleria by DFS: Indulge in tax-free shopping at The Galleria by DFS, a haven for luxury brands, cosmetics, accessories, and fine jewelry . As a DFS Rewards member, enjoy personalized service, exclusive promotions, and VIP treatment.

Pedder Building: Step into a historic landmark transformed into a haven for upscale fashion. Explore the Pedder Building's unique architecture and discover designer showrooms showcasing the latest collections from renowned names and emerging talents .

Landmark Prince's: For the epitome of luxury shopping, visit Landmark Prince's. This exclusive arcade offers high-end fashion, accessories, and lifestyle brands, from luxury watches and designer clothing to leather goods . Expect sophisticated shopping and personalized service.

On Lan Street: Embrace chic and trendy vibes on On Lan Street. This enclave features a captivating mix of luxury boutiques, concept stores, and flagship stores from international brands . Discover the latest trends in fashion, beauty, and lifestyle, all complemented by stylish cafes and eateries.

Lee Tung Avenue: Venture beyond Central to Lee Tung Avenue, a luxury haven in Wan Chai. Explore this tree-lined boulevard featuring a curated selection of luxury boutiques, fine dining establishments, and upscale lifestyle amenities. Immerse yourself in a sophisticated and cosmopolitan shopping experience .

Nightlife hotspots

Hong Kong transforms into a dazzling metropolis after dark. From energetic bars to rooftop havens with city views, here's where the city comes alive:

Lan Kwai Fong: Central's beating heart of nightlife, Lan Kwai Fong boasts a vibrant atmosphere, bustling bars, and energetic crowds. Dive into pubs, clubs, and restaurants offering live music, DJs, themed parties, and international cuisine.

Soho: A stone's throw away, Soho (South of Hollywood Road) is known for its trendy bars, hip cafes, and eclectic dining. Explore hidden gems, speakeasies, and rooftop bars with stunning cityscapes. Soho's laid-back vibe caters to locals and expats alike.

Wan Chai: This vibrant neighborhood offers an eclectic mix of bars, clubs, and entertainment venues. Explore Lockhart Road, Jaffe Road, and surrounding areas to discover traditional pubs, karaoke lounges, upscale cocktail bars, and live music experiences.

Tsim Sha Tsui: Kowloon's bustling Tsim Sha Tsui district offers vibrant nightlife and entertainment. Visit Knutsford Terrace for al fresco dining and lively bars, or explore the waterfront promenade for stunning Victoria Harbour views. Rooftop bars, live music venues, and international clubs provide diverse experiences.

Happy Valley Racecourse: Immerse yourself in the excitement of horse racing under the stars at Happy Valley Racecourse. Enjoy the electrifying atmosphere, place your bets, and soak up the energy of this iconic Hong Kong tradition. Live music and entertainment options make it a memorable night out.

Rooftop Bars: Admire Hong Kong's dazzling skyline from rooftop bars. Options like Ozone at The Ritz-Carlton, Aqua Spirit in Tsim Sha Tsui, and SEVVA in Central offer panoramic views, signature cocktails, and chic ambiance. Perfect for a romantic date or a night out with friends.

Central District: Beyond luxury shopping and dining, Central offers a vibrant nightlife scene. Peel Street and Staunton Street are havens for trendy bars, speakeasies, and cocktail lounges hidden within historic buildings. Find intimate wine bars or lively pubs - there's something for everyone.

Stunning Views by Night: Enjoy a unique experience with stunning views at the Hong Kong Observation Wheel and AIA Vitality Park. Take a leisurely ride on the wheel, admire the city's illuminated skyline, then relax in the park with food and drinks from nearby vendors. A serene and memorable way to spend an evening.

Sing Your Heart Out: Karaoke, or "KTV," is a popular pastime. Head to Tsim Sha Tsui, Causeway Bay, or Mong Kok for karaoke bars with private rooms, extensive song selections, and drinks packages. It's a night of singing and entertainment with friends!

Laughter is the Best Medicine: Catch the Hong Kong International Comedy Festival for a night of laughs. Local and international comedians perform stand-up, improv, and sketch shows at various venues across the city. Enjoy an evening of comedy and camaraderie.

Night Markets After Dark: While most street markets operate during the day, some extend their hours. Explore Temple Street Night Market for a lively atmosphere, street food vendors, and stalls with everything from clothing to souvenirs.

Late-Night Eats: Hong Kong's vibrant food scene extends into the night. Many restaurants, cafes, and eateries stay open late, offering a variety of cuisines. Whether you crave dim sum, late-night noodles, or international fare, you'll find the perfect fuel for your nightlife adventures.

Cultural performances and events

Hong Kong offers a vibrant cultural scene with a range of performances and events throughout the year. Here's a glimpse into what awaits you:

Hong Kong Cultural Centre: This premier venue stages a variety of music, dance, theater, and opera productions. From the Hong Kong Philharmonic Orchestra to the Hong Kong Ballet, experience world-class performances by local and international artists.

Hong Kong Arts Festival: This annual event features a rich program of performances and exhibitions across various art forms. Witness classical music concerts, opera productions, contemporary dance, and theater productions, celebrating the diversity of Hong Kong's arts scene.

Chinese Opera: Explore the rich tradition of Chinese opera with captivating performances at venues like the Sunbeam Theatre and Yau Ma Tei Theatre. Witness elaborate costumes, makeup, intricate choreography, and storytelling, offering a glimpse into Chinese culture and heritage.

Lunar New Year: Celebrate the arrival of Lunar New Year with vibrant festivities. Experience traditional lion dances, dragon boat races, street parades, and firework displays as the city ushers in the new year with joy and color.

Mid-Autumn Festival: Join the festivities of the Mid-Autumn Festival. Enjoy lantern displays, mooncake tastings, and traditional performances at Victoria Park and Tsim Sha Tsui Promenade. Celebrate under the moonlit sky with cultural activities perfect for families.

Chinese New Year Night Parade: Witness the spectacle of the Chinese New Year Night Parade. Tsim Sha Tsui comes alive with colorful floats, marching bands, lion and dragon dances, and cultural performances. Celebrate the new year with music, dance, and a festive atmosphere.

Hong Kong International Film Festival: This prestigious film event showcases a diverse selection of local and international films, documentaries, and shorts. Enjoy world premieres, retrospectives, industry forums, and filmmaker Q&A sessions, celebrating the art of cinema.

Cultural Workshops and Demonstrations: Delve into traditional arts and crafts with cultural workshops. Learn Chinese calligraphy, brush painting, or tea appreciation at cultural centers, museums, and heritage sites. Gain hands-on experience and insights into Chinese culture and traditions.

CHAPTER NINE

DAY TRIPS AND EXCURSIONS

Hong Kong's bustling energy is contagious, but sometimes you crave a change of pace. Look no further! Here are exciting day trips to broaden your horizons:

Lantau Island:

Trade cityscapes for serenity on Lantau Island. Ascend Ngong Ping 360 for breathtaking island views, marvel at the Tian Tan Buddha (Big Buddha), and explore the Po Lin Monastery. Immerse yourself in cultural immersion, natural beauty, and scenic hikes on Ngong Ping Village and the Wisdom Path.

Macau:

Embark on a day trip to Macau, a captivating blend of Portuguese and Chinese cultures. Explore UNESCO-listed gems like the Ruins of St. Paul's, Senado Square, and A-Ma Temple. Delight in Macau's culinary scene with Portuguese egg tarts and Macanese cuisine. Try your luck at the city's casinos or be dazzled by extravagant resort shows.

Shenzhen:

Journey to mainland China's dynamic Shenzhen. Witness futuristic architecture, bustling markets, and cultural gems like Splendid China Folk Village and Window of the World. Explore shopping havens like Huaqiangbei Electronics Market and Luohu Commercial City, or be inspired by local artists at Dafen Oil Painting Village. Experience the rapid development and energy of this modern metropolis.

Mui Wo and Silvermine Bay Beach:

Lantau Island's southern coast beckons with natural beauty. Take a ferry to Mui Wo, a charming waterfront village with a laid-back vibe and scenic hikes. Relax on the golden sands of Silvermine Bay Beach, swim in clear waters, or kayak along the picturesque coastline. Savor fresh seafood and unwind in the serene ambiance of this seaside escape.

Tai O Fishing Village:

Discover the rustic charm of Tai O Fishing Village. Explore traditional stilt houses, bustling markets, and scenic waterways on a boat ride. Alternatively, wander through historic streets and visit cultural landmarks like the Tai O Heritage Hotel and Yeung Hau Temple. Sample unique local delicacies and immerse yourself in the village's way of life.

Cheung Chau Island:

Escape to the car-free island paradise of Cheung Chau. Take a ferry and discover scenic beaches, hiking trails, and traditional fishing villages. Explore iconic attractions like Pak Tai Temple, Cheung Po Tsai Cave, and Tung Wan Beach. Rent a bicycle for a scenic coastal ride and savor fresh seafood at waterfront restaurants.

Macau day trip

Macau awaits! This vibrant city, a unique blend of Portuguese and Chinese influences, offers a captivating day trip from Hong Kong. Here's your itinerary to maximize your Macau adventure:

The Journey Begins (1 hour):

Take a ferry from Hong Kong's China Ferry Terminal or Hong Kong-Macau Ferry Terminal. Ferries depart regularly, whisking you away to Macau in about an hour.

Step Back in Time (Morning):

Upon arrival, delve into Macau's historic city center, a UNESCO World Heritage Site. Explore its charming cobblestone streets and marvel at the well-preserved colonial architecture.

Ruins of St. Paul's: Witness the iconic Ruins of St. Paul's, a 16th-century church facade standing after a fire.

Senado Square: Stroll through Senado Square, the lively heart of the historic district. Admire the pastel buildings, shop for souvenirs, and indulge in Macau's famous street food like Portuguese egg tarts and almond cookies.

A-Ma Temple: Discover Macau's rich maritime history at the A-Ma Temple, one of the oldest temples dedicated to the sea goddess Mazu. Explore its intricate architecture and serene courtyards.

A Culinary Adventure (Lunch):

Treat yourself to Macanese cuisine, a delicious fusion of Portuguese and Chinese flavors. Savor dishes like baked codfish, African chicken, or seafood rice, paired with Portuguese wine or Macau's almond liqueur.

Modern Marvels and Thrill Seeks (Afternoon):

Ascend the Macau Tower for breathtaking panoramic views. Take the high-speed elevator to the observation deck and admire the city, the Pearl River Delta, and beyond. Feeling adventurous? Try the Skywalk or take the plunge with a bungee jump!

Casino Visit: Experience the glitz and glamour of Macau's casinos. Explore the gaming floors, entertainment complexes, and extravagant interiors of iconic establishments like The Venetian Macao, Wynn Macau, or MGM Macau.

Evening Entertainment:

As the day winds down, immerse yourself in Macau's entertainment scene. From world-class concerts and theatrical productions to mesmerizing water shows and vibrant nightlife, there's something for everyone.

Return to Hong Kong (Evening):

Board the ferry back to Hong Kong, reflecting on your memorable day trip filled with cultural encounters, historical exploration, and a touch of excitement.

Shenzhen day trip

Shenzhen beckons! This dynamic city, known for its rapid growth, futuristic skyline, and cultural gems, is a perfect day trip from Hong Kong. Here's your itinerary to maximize your Shenzhen adventure:

The Journey Begins (1 hour):

Take a high-speed train or a convenient cross-border bus from Hong Kong. The trip takes about an hour, depending on your chosen mode of transport.

Modern Marvels (Morning):

Upon arrival, immerse yourself in Shenzhen's modern marvels. Visit the architectural wonders of Shenzhen Civic Center or the impressive Shenzhen Bay Sports

Center. Marvel at the contemporary design and soak up the energy of this bustling metropolis.

Cultural Gems (Afternoon):

Splendid China Folk Village: Step into a miniature China! Explore the Splendid China Folk Village, a vast park showcasing replicas of China's iconic landmarks, historical sites, and ethnic villages. Wander through intricate exhibits like the Great Wall, Forbidden City, and Terracotta Army, gaining insights into China's diverse regions.

Window of the World: Travel the world in a day! Visit the Window of the World, a theme park featuring scaled-down replicas of global landmarks. Marvel at the Eiffel Tower, Taj Mahal, and Egyptian pyramids. Enjoy interactive exhibits, cultural shows, and thrilling rides - a fun experience for all ages.

A Culinary Adventure (Lunch):

Treat your taste buds to authentic Cantonese cuisine and regional specialties at a local Shenzhen restaurant. Savor dim sum, roasted meats, seafood dishes, and flavorful stir-fries, all accompanied by traditional Chinese tea.

Shopping Escapades (Afternoon):

Huaqiangbei Electronics Market: Gear up for the latest technology! Explore the vast Huaqiangbei Electronics Market, one of the world's largest. Browse countless stalls selling gadgets, components, and accessories - from smartphones to drones, you'll find it all here!

Dafen Oil Painting Village: Immerse yourself in art! Visit the Dafen Oil Painting Village, a renowned artist community known for its high-quality oil paintings and reproductions. Witness local artists at work and explore galleries brimming with masterpieces. Purchase unique souvenirs - original artworks or commissioned pieces to remember your Shenzhen visit.

Luohu Commercial City: Shop till you drop! End your day with a shopping spree at Luohu Commercial City. Explore a bustling complex offering a vast selection of goods at bargain prices. From clothes and accessories to electronics and souvenirs, find everything you need. Hone your haggling skills to score the best deals!

Return to Hong Kong (Evening):

Take a high-speed train or cross-border bus back to Hong Kong, reminiscing about your day trip filled with cultural discoveries, modern wonders, and shopping sprees.

Outlying islands (Lamma Island, Cheung Chau)

Hong Kong is a city that thrives on energy, but sometimes you crave a tranquil escape. Look no further than the outlying islands! Lamma Island and Cheung Chau offer a day trip filled with natural beauty, cultural charm, and serene beaches. Here's your itinerary to experience these idyllic island paradises:

The Journey Begins (25-40 minutes):

Take a ferry from Central Pier in Hong Kong to Yung Shue Wan or Sok Kwu Wan on Lamma Island. Ferries depart regularly throughout the day, and the journey takes approximately 25-30 minutes.

Lamma Island: Serenity and Seafood (Morning - Afternoon)

Upon arrival on Lamma Island, start your day exploring. Depending on which ferry pier you arrive at, you can choose to explore Yung Shue Wan in the north or Sok Kwu Wan in the south.

Scenic Hike: Lace up your boots and embark on a scenic hike along Lamma Island's picturesque trails. The Lamma Island Family Trail offers panoramic views with plenty of opportunities to spot local wildlife and enjoy the tranquility of nature.

Seafood Lunch: Indulge in a seafood feast at one of the island's waterfront restaurants in Sok Kwu Wan, known for its fresh seafood and alfresco dining atmosphere. Savor the flavors of the sea while overlooking the harbor.

Beach Time: After lunch, relax and unwind on one of Lamma Island's scenic beaches. Head to Hung Shing Yeh Beach near Yung Shue Wan or Lo So Shing Beach near Sok Kwu Wan to soak up the sun, swim in the clear waters, or simply lounge on the sand with a good book.

Explore the Villages: Take a leisurely stroll through the charming villages of Yung Shue Wan and Sok Kwu Wan. Discover traditional stilt houses, local shops, and colorful street art. Immerse yourself in the island's laid-back ambiance.

Cheung Chau: Temples, Beaches, and Buns (Afternoon - Evening)

Take a ferry from Yung Shue Wan or Sok Kwu Wan to Cheung Chau, another picturesque island known for its sandy beaches, seafood restaurants, and annual Bun Festival. Ferries operate regularly, with a short journey time of approximately 30-40 minutes.

Explore Cheung Chau: Upon arrival, explore the island's bustling harbor, historic temples, and scenic promenades. Rent a bicycle or explore on foot as you make your way to the island's main attractions.

Pak Tai Temple: Visit Pak Tai Temple, a centuries-old Taoist temple dedicated to the Sea God. Admire the temple's architecture, carvings, and decorations, and learn about its cultural significance.

Tung Wan Beach: Spend some time relaxing on Tung Wan Beach, one of Cheung Chau's most popular beaches. Enjoy swimming, sunbathing, or beach volleyball, and take in the serene ambiance.

Wandering the Streets: Wander through the narrow streets and alleyways of Cheung Chau's old town. Find traditional seafood restaurants, souvenir shops, and street food vendors selling local delicacies.

Return to Hong Kong (Evening):

After a day of exploration and relaxation, take the ferry back to Hong Kong from Cheung Chau. Reflect on your island adventure and the natural beauty and cultural charm you've experienced.

Historical sites in New Territories

The New Territories offer a glimpse into Hong Kong's rich history and cultural heritage. Here are 20 historical sites not to miss:

Lung Yeuk Tau Heritage Trail: Discover ancient villages, walled compounds, and ancestral halls along this scenic trail, which highlights the heritage of the Tang Clan and other prominent Hakka families.

Ping Shan Heritage Trail: Explore historic landmarks such as the Ping Shan Tang Clan Gallery cum Heritage Trail Visitors Centre, Tang Ancestral Hall, and Tsui Sing Lau Pagoda, showcasing the heritage of the Tang Clan.

Che Kung Temple: Pay homage to Che Kung, a military commander revered for his ability to suppress plagues and bring good fortune, at this centuries-old temple in Sha Tin.

Man Mo Temple, Tai Po: Visit this traditional Chinese temple dedicated to the gods of literature (Man) and war (Mo), located in Tai Po Market, and admire its intricate architectural details and ornate decorations.

Tai Fu Tai Mansion: Step back in time at this beautifully preserved Qing dynasty mansion in San Tin, featuring elaborate wood carvings, painted ceilings, and a tranquil garden courtyard.

Tin Hau Temple, Yuen Long: Worship at this ancient temple dedicated to Tin Hau, the Goddess of the Sea, and explore its historic architecture and cultural significance to the local fishing community.

Sam Tung Uk Museum: Learn about the history of the Hakka people and traditional rural life in the New

Territories at this restored Hakka walled village in Tsuen Wan, now converted into a museum.

Wong Tai Sin Temple: Seek blessings and divine guidance at one of Hong Kong's most famous Taoist temples, dedicated to Wong Tai Sin, the Great Immortal Wong.

Hong Kong Heritage Museum: Explore the rich cultural heritage of Hong Kong through interactive exhibitions, artifacts, and multimedia displays at this state-of-the-art museum in Sha Tin.

Kowloon Walled City Park: Wander through the tranquil gardens and remnants of the former Kowloon Walled City, once a densely populated urban enclave notorious for its lawlessness and unique architecture.

Tin Hau Temple, Tin Shui Wai (Temple dedicated to the Goddess of the Sea)

Tai Wo Hau Village (Traditional walled village with ancestral halls and fortified walls)

Kwu Tung Study Hall (Historic study hall for Confucian teachings)

Tsz Shan Monastery (Modern Buddhist monastery with a towering Guanyin statue)

Hong Kong Railway Museum (Exhibits on Hong Kong's railway history in a former train station)

Kai Tak Cruise Terminal (Site of the former Kai Tak Airport with a modern cruise terminal)

Lai Chi Kok Park (Scenic park with landscaped gardens, jogging trails, and recreational facilities)

Tin Hau Temple, Tai Po (Historic temple dedicated to the Goddess of the Sea)

Tai Po Market (Bustling market town with fresh produce, local delicacies, and handmade crafts)

Yuen Long Park (Expansive park with lush greenery, scenic ponds, and jogging trails)

Lung Kwu Tan Village (Historic fishing village with stilt houses, seafood restaurants, and waterfront views)

Hong Kong Correctional Services Museum (Museum on Hong Kong's correctional system in a former prison)

Tuen Mun Town Plaza (Large shopping mall with a variety of stores, restaurants, and entertainment)

Tung Chung Fort (Remnants of a historic fort with panoramic coastal views)

Sai Kung Old Town (Former fishing village with seafood restaurants, waterfront promenades, and boat tours)

CHAPTER TEN

CONCLUSION AND ADDITIONAL RESOURCES

The New Territories beckon, offering a captivating journey through time. Here, ancient traditions, colonial echoes, and modern marvels intertwine, creating a unique cultural tapestry.

A Treasure Trove of History

Embark on a historical expedition and discover a treasure trove waiting to be unearthed. Explore centuries-old temples, like the Tin Hau Temples dedicated to the Goddess of the Sea, standing as testaments to the region's maritime heritage. Witness the grandeur of ancestral halls and fortified villages, whispering tales of bygone eras. Unveil the architectural beauty of historic landmarks like the Tai Fu Tai Mansion, a Qing dynasty masterpiece.

Beyond Monuments: Unveiling Cultural Gems

Venture beyond the imposing structures and delve into the heart of the New Territories' cultural soul. Explore the vibrant markets of Tai Po, teeming with fresh produce and local crafts. Immerse yourself in the serenity of Tsz Shan Monastery, a modern Buddhist haven. Learn about the region's correctional past at the Hong Kong Correctional Services Museum.

A Journey Through Time

Whether you wander through the tranquil gardens of the Kowloon Walled City Park, a transformed enclave, or hike the Lung Yeuk Tau Heritage Trail, uncovering the legacy of the Tang Clan, each experience offers a unique chapter in the story of the New Territories.

Planning Your Exploration

To fully enrich your historical adventure, consider these resources:

Hong Kong Tourism Board (HKTB): (https://www.discoverhongkong.com) - Your one-stop shop for travel planning, including attractions and itineraries in the New Territories.

Antiquities and Monuments Office (AMO): (https://www.amo.gov.hk/en/) - Explore heritage trails, conservation projects, and learn about historic sites.

Museum of History, Hong Kong: (https://www.lcsd.gov.hk/en/mh/index.html) - Delve deeper into Hong Kong's history, with a focus on the New Territories, through interactive exhibits.

Heritage Trails of Hong Kong: (https://www.heritagetrails.hk) - Uncover hidden gems through themed trails that highlight cultural landmarks and scenic landscapes.

Local Tour Operators: - Gain local insights and personalized experiences by joining a guided tour led by experts.

Final thoughts on visiting Hong Kong

Hong Kong beckons with a promise of an unforgettable experience. Here, the pulse of a modern metropolis throbs alongside the serenity of nature, offering a captivating blend for every traveler.

A City That Captivates All Senses

Soar to new heights atop Victoria Peak and marvel at the city's dazzling skyline. Immerse yourself in the cacophony of street markets overflowing with vibrant sights, enticing aromas, and delectable treats. Savor the city's rich culinary tapestry, from delicate dim sum to Michelin-starred delights. Explore ancient temples whispering tales of a bygone era, and delve into the heart of cultural districts brimming with energy.

Beyond the Neon Lights: A Haven for Nature Lovers

Escape the urban buzz and discover Hong Kong's hidden natural gems. Hike along scenic trails, bask on pristine beaches on outlying islands, or embark on a tranquil boat ride through the Victoria Harbour, soaking in the city's beauty from a unique perspective.

A Blend of East and West: A Cultural Tapestry

Hong Kong's unique position as a global hub fosters a fascinating fusion of cultures. Witness the harmonious blend of Eastern traditions and Western influences that permeate the city's architecture, cuisine, and customs.

Travel Tips: Planning Your Hong Kong Adventure

Stay Informed: Be mindful of Hong Kong's current political and social landscape, and consult travel advisories for the latest safety precautions.

Respect Local Customs: Embrace the cultural nuances and traditions to ensure a smooth and respectful visit.

Explore Responsibly: Exercise caution in unfamiliar areas and prioritize your safety throughout your exploration.

A City Awaits: Unleash Your Inner Explorer

Hong Kong promises a treasure trove of experiences waiting to be discovered. Whether you crave historical immersion, culinary adventures, or outdoor escapades, this dynamic city caters to all.

Useful websites and apps for travelers

Planning a trip to Hong Kong? Look no further! This essential toolkit equips you with the best apps and websites to navigate the city, discover hidden gems, and make the most of your Hong Kong adventure.

Navigation and Getting Around:

Google Maps: Your trusty companion for navigating Hong Kong's bustling streets. Get real-time traffic updates, public transportation information, and explore hidden alleys with ease.

MTR Mobile: The official app for Hong Kong's efficient Mass Transit Railway (MTR) system. Plan your routes, check fares, and access station maps for seamless travel across the city.

HKTaxi: Hail a cab with ease! Book, track, and pay for taxi rides directly through this app, eliminating the hassle of navigating unfamiliar streets.

Accommodation and Booking:

Booking.com: Find your perfect stay in Hong Kong, from luxurious hotels to budget-friendly guesthouses. Browse a wide range of options and secure your booking in advance.

Airbnb: Experience a unique perspective of the city by staying in apartments, homestays, or private rooms offered on Airbnb. Discover hidden gems and potentially save on accommodation costs.

Dining and Activities:

TripAdvisor: Read reviews, discover top-rated restaurants, and explore exciting activities in Hong Kong. Find hidden gems and must-see attractions based on real traveler experiences.

OpenRice: Foodies rejoice! This platform is your one-stop shop for exploring Hong Kong's diverse culinary scene. Discover authentic Cantonese and Chinese fare, or delve into international cuisine options.

Klook: Book tours, activities, and attraction tickets at discounted prices. Skip the lines, secure hassle-free travel packages, and unlock unique experiences in Hong Kong.

Planning and Information:

Hong Kong Tourism Board (HKTB): The official HKTB website is your comprehensive guide to all things Hong Kong. Discover attractions, events, transportation options, and insider tips for planning your itinerary.

Hong Kong Government e-Service: Stay informed and prepared with access to visa information, immigration procedures, emergency contacts, and travel advisories directly from the Hong Kong government.

Hong Kong Observatory: Check the official Hong Kong Observatory website or app for up-to-date weather forecasts, typhoon warnings, and weather advisories. Ensure you pack accordingly and plan activities based on real-time weather conditions.

Bonus Apps:

HK Express: The official app of HK Express, a budget airline, allows you to search for flights, book tickets, manage bookings, and check-in online for a smooth travel experience to or from Hong Kong.

Travel Tip: Download essential information and maps offline before your trip to ensure you have access to them even without an internet connection.

Further reading and references

Lonely Planet Hong Kong: Your one-stop guide for navigating Hong Kong's vibrant streets, from hidden gems to must-see attractions.

Rough Guides: Hong Kong: Unravel the city's rich tapestry with detailed historical and cultural insights, alongside practical travel tips.

Fodor's Essential Hong Kong: Curated recommendations and itineraries ensure you experience the best of Hong Kong's offerings.

Beyond the Tourist Trail: Books for the Curious Mind

Hong Kong: Culture and the Politics of Disappearance by Ackbar Abbas: Explore the complexities of Hong Kong's identity and its place in the globalized world.

Hong Kong: A Cultural History by Michael Ingham: Delve into the city's fascinating cultural evolution, from its colonial roots to its present-day vibrancy.

City of Protest: A Recent History of Dissent in Hong Kong by Antony Dapiran: Gain an understanding of Hong Kong's fight for democracy and its history of activism.

Experiences that Enrich:

Hong Kong Heritage Discovery Centre: Uncover Hong Kong's past through interactive exhibits, workshops, and historical artifacts.

Hong Kong Museum of History: Embark on a chronological journey through Hong Kong's history, from prehistoric times to its modern transformation.

Hong Kong Heritage Conservation Foundation: Immerse yourself in the city's architectural legacy through resources and educational programs.

Your Gateway to Exploration:

Hong Kong Tourism Board (HKTB) website: The HKTB website remains your dependable resource for planning and exploration. Find interactive maps, downloadable resources, and up-to-date travel information.

News and Current Affairs:

Hong Kong Free Press: (https://hongkongfp.com/) - Independent news covering local events, politics, and social issues.

South China Morning Post: (https://www.scmp.com/asia) - Leading English newspaper with comprehensive coverage of local and international news.

Academic Exploration:

Hong Kong University Press: (https://hkupress.hku.hk/) - Scholarly works and research publications on Hong Kong studies.

Hong Kong Studies Association: (https://hkstudies.org/) - Promotes research and scholarship on Hong Kong's history, society, and culture.

Business and Economics:

Hong Kong Economic Journal: (https://hkej.com/) - Financial news focusing on business, economics, and financial markets in Hong Kong and Greater China.

Local Perspectives:

Hong Kong Public Libraries: (https://www.hkpl.gov.hk/) - Extensive collection of books and resources on Hong Kong's history, culture, and society.

Cultural Gems:

Hong Kong Arts Centre: (https://hkac.org.hk/) - Diverse cultural programs, exhibitions, and events showcasing contemporary art, film, and performing arts.

Hong Kong Design Institute (HKDI): (https://hkdi.edu.hk/) - Discover innovative design work through exhibitions and programs focusing on design education.

Hong Kong International Literary Festival: (https://www.instagram.com/litfest_hk/?hl=en) -

Annual festival celebrating literature with readings, discussions, and book signings by renowned authors.

A Glimpse into the Past:

Hong Kong Tourism History Archive: (https://digitalrepository.lib.hku.hk/hktbc) - Unveils the city's past as a tourist destination through vintage travel materials.

Made in the USA
Las Vegas, NV
14 November 2024

11800548R00098